C000257317

FOUL DEEDS AND SUSPICIOUS
DEATHS IN CROYDON

FOUL DEEDS AND SUSPICIOUS DEATHS Series

Wharncliffe's *Foul Deeds and Suspicious Deaths* series explores, in detail, crimes of passion, brutal murders and foul misdemeanours from early modern times to the present day. Victorian street crime, mysterious death and modern murders tell tales where passion, jealousy and social deprivation brought unexpected violence to those involved. From unexplained death and suicide to murder and manslaughter, the books provide a fascinating insight into the lives of both victims and perpetrators as well as society as a whole.

Other titles in the series include:

Foul Deeds and Suspicious Deaths in Birmingham, Nick Billingham
ISBN: 1-903425-96-4. £10.99

Foul Deeds and Suspicious Deaths in Bolton, Glynis Cooper
ISBN: 1-903425-63-8. £9.99

Foul Deeds and Suspicious Deaths in Colchester, Patrick Denney
ISBN: 1-903425-80-8. £10.99

Foul Deeds and Suspicious Deaths in Coventry, David McGrory
ISBN: 1-903425-57-3. £9.99

Foul Deeds and Suspicious Deaths Around Derby, Kevin Turton
ISBN: 1-903425-76-X. £9.99

Foul Deeds and Suspicious Deaths in and around Durham, Maureen Anderson
ISBN: 1-903425-46-8. £9.99

Foul Deeds and Suspicious Deaths in London's East End, Geoffrey Howse
ISBN: 1-903425-71-9. £10.99

Foul Deeds and Suspicious Deaths in Hampstead, Holborn & St Pancras,
Mark Aston
ISBN: 1-903425-94-8. £10.99

Foul Deeds and Suspicious Deaths in Hull, David Goodman
ISBN: 1-903425-43-3. £9.99

Foul Deeds and Suspicious Deaths Around Leicester, Kevin Turton
ISBN: 1-903425-75-1. £10.99

Foul Deeds and Suspicious Deaths in Manchester, Martin Baggoley
ISBN: 1-903425-65-4. £9.99

Foul Deeds and Suspicious Deaths in Newcastle, Maureen Anderson
ISBN: 1-903425-34-4. £9.99

Foul Deeds and Suspicious Deaths in Newport, Terry Underwood
ISBN: 1-903425-59-X. £9.99

Foul Deeds and Suspicious Deaths in and Around Scunthorpe, Stephen Wade
ISBN: 1-903425-88-3. £9.99

More Foul Deeds and Suspicious Deaths in Wakefield, Kate Taylor
ISBN: 1-903425-48-4. £9.99

Foul Deeds and Suspicious Deaths in York, Keith Henson
ISBN: 1-903425-33-6. £9.99

Foul Deeds and Suspicious Deaths on the Yorkshire Coast, Alan Whitworth
ISBN: 1-903425-01-8. £9.99

Please contact us via any of the methods below for more information or a catalogue.

WHARNCLIFFE BOOKS

47 Church Street – Barnsley – South Yorkshire – S70 2AS

Tel: 01226 734555 – 734222 Fax: 01226 734438

E-mail: enquiries@pen-and-sword.co.uk – Website: www.wharncliffebooks.co.uk

Foul Deeds & Suspicious Deaths In
CROYDON

Caroline Maxton

Series Editor
Brian Elliott

Wharncliffe Books

First published in Great Britain in 2006 by
Wharncliffe Local History
an imprint of
Pen & Sword Books Ltd
47 Church Street
Barnsley
South Yorkshire
S70 2AS

Copyright (c) Caroline Maxton, 2006

ISBN 1 84563 007 6

The right of Caroline Maxton to be identified as Authors
of the Work has been asserted by her in accordance with
the Copyright, Designs and Patents Act 1988.

A CIP catalogue record for this book is available from the
British Library

All rights reserved. No part of this book may be
reproduced or transmitted in any form or by any means,
electronic or mechanical including photocopying,
recording or by any information storage and retrieval
system, without permission from the Publisher in writing.

Typeset in Plantin and Benguiat by
[Phoenix Typesetting, Auldgirth, Dumfriesshire

Printed and bound in England by
CPI UK

Pen & Sword Books Ltd incorporates the Imprints of Pen
& Sword Aviation, Pen & Sword Maritime,
Pen & Sword Military, Wharncliffe Local History, Pen
and Sword Select, Pen and Sword Military Classics and
Leo Cooper.

For a complete list of Pen & Sword titles please contact
PEN & SWORD BOOKS LIMITED
47 Church Street
Barnsley
South Yorkshire
S70 2AS, England
E-mail: enquiries@pen-and-sword.co.uk
Website: www.pen-and-sword.co.uk

Contents

For My Mother
who helps with everything

Acknowledgements

It is impossible to complete the research for a book like this without a great deal of help. I am indebted to the staff of various research centres, including the British Library and the National Archives. But my special thanks go to the staff of the Croydon Local Studies Library, not only for their patience and efficiency, but for going to extraordinary lengths to help with all my enquiries, sometimes providing the answer before I'd even managed to work out the question!

And then there are the many individuals who helped along the way. My thanks go to Jim Brown for providing technical know-how for the illustrations; to Dr Malcolm Cooper, Mary and Richard Mobbs and Norah Adams for their sharp eyes in reading the manuscript, and for knowing just how to turn a phrase to make it right; to Louise Ferns, Sarah Lott and Marion Brown for all their hard work and enthusiasm in the research; and to Robert Grant for finding George Guy, John O'Leary and many of the photographs, for his insight in reading the manuscript, but most of all for keeping the smile on my face.

Croydon Local Studies Library

Introduction

his is a book about murder. It is the story of both murderers and victims, and it is the story of the circumstances that led them to their place in history.

Within the closest relationships we find the highest levels of emotion and tension, and nowhere is this more evident than within the family unit. In this collection of personal histories so many tales of murder emerge from within the heart of the family: men killing the women they love in a fit of passion, parents murdering their children, lost in their own despair. The relationships are complex, the protagonists often hard to understand, but their problems are universal: the struggle to make ends meet, jealousy, greed, miscommunication. We recognize them all.

Many of the stories are wrapped in mystery. We may know

Metropolitan Special Constabulary, Croydon Sub-division 1918. Croydon Local Studies Library

The Old Jail, Surrey Street. Croydon Local Studies Library

Prisoners at East Croydon Station, handcuffed. Croydon Local Studies Library

what happened, but not why; in at least three of the cases even the murderers were unable to explain their actions. The story of Miles Vallint remains unsolved, and in the Birdhurst Rise poisonings there are many more questions than answers.

The tales of foul deeds span a period of more than two hundred years, and the locations will be familiar to all those living in and around the Croydon area. The town experienced an enormous period of growth in the nineteenth century, the population swelling from 6,742 to 141,918 between 1801 and 1901. With this came the inevitable overcrowding and poverty, and many of the earlier cases occurred in the poorest parts of the town. But affluence, too, carries a price, as we see in the stories of John Shippey and Gordon Eric Gordon-Tombe.

But it is not just the dark side of humanity that reveals itself here. Close family unity, community support and compassion are there too, sometimes shown in ways that take our breath away. The mother of murder victim Carol Soan leads the way in this.

Some of the stories are famous, inspiring books, documentaries and films. Others may be quite unfamiliar. They are all sad. In each we see ordinary people living ordinary lives, struggling with their personal difficulties within the context of their time.

CHAPTER 1

The Birdhurst Rise Mysteries:
Edmund Duff, 1928
Vera and Violet Sidney, 1929

Who can say who did it?

Under the cover of darkness, two bodies were exhumed from the Queen's Road Cemetery, Croydon. The press had been following this particular case closely, and police wished to remove the bodies to the mortuary at Mayday Hospital before news of the exhumations broke. Standing at the graveside was Tom Sidney, and it fell to him to identify the bodies of his mother, Violet, and his sister, Vera, by the light of the hurricane lamps. It was March 1929.

Less than eight weeks later, on 18 May, Tom was back at the cemetery in the early hours of the morning to identify his brother-in-law, Edmund Duff. But this time he was called on to do nothing more than confirm the nameplate on the coffin. The police were opening an investigation into three separate deaths that had occurred within one family in the space of eleven months and there were whispered rumours of murder.

Although not conspicuously wealthy, the Sidney family had lived quite comfortably. Sixty-eight-year-old Violet was the widow of Thomas Sidney, an eminent barrister, and she lived with her forty-year-old spinster daughter, Vera, at 29 Birdhurst Rise, South Croydon. It was a Victorian house, generous in size and graceful in appearance, and properly reflected the respectability of its occupants. Violet's other two children, Tom and Grace, lived nearby. It was a close family, drawn closer still by the departure of their father, Thomas Sidney, who ran off to India with his brother's sister-in-law. It was not the first of his affairs and Violet's anger at her husband's infidelity burned brightly for the remainder of her life.

On their father's death in 1917 Grace, Vera and Tom received absolutely nothing from his will, but his passing meant they were now each entitled to £5,000 from a legacy set up by their paternal grandfather. Thomas Sidney might have fallen short in his duties as a father, but before his death he did one thing that had a great impact on Grace's life – he introduced her to her future husband.

Transfer of Edmund Duff's body following exhumation. Second from the left of the group following the hearse is Tom Sidney.
Hulton Picture Library

Thomas Sidney had met Edmund Duff in India, and they struck up an easy friendship that continued after their return to England. When Thomas introduced Duff to his twenty-three-year-old daughter in 1909 he had no idea that they would marry two years later. It was a seemingly happy marriage. Grace and Edmund had five children together, although they suffered the sadness of losing two of them in infancy. Not everyone approved of the union, however. Edmund was seventeen years older than Grace, not good with money and was disapproved of by Violet. She always found it difficult to accept into her family a man who was a close friend of the husband who had abandoned her.

Edmund Duff worked in the Colonial Service, and later for the Ministry of Pensions, but had lost his post by the mid-1920s. Although he earned relatively small sums from a clerical job and from writing articles and short stories, the shortage of money in the Duff branch of the family became yet another issue of which Violet disapproved. Grace herself took a more philosophical approach: what they lacked in prosperity they made up for in family affection, and the odd threadbare patch in their home at 16 South Park Road was overlooked.

On 26 April 1928 Edmund came home from a short fishing trip in Fordingbridge, Hampshire. He generally enjoyed good health, but on the journey back had started to feel unwell: he was shivering and slightly feverish, but Grace was not unduly concerned. Like many other normally robust people, Edmund tended to exaggerate any minor ailments, and besides he looked quite well. Grace and the children had already eaten, but there was a meal of chicken and potatoes and Edmund's favourite beer waiting for him on his return. He ate very little of the food, but drank the beer. Later that evening he began to feel worse, and so Grace called Dr Robert Elwell to see her husband. There was nothing obviously amiss other than a slightly raised temperature and nausea. The doctor recommended taking aspirin and quinine, and as much rest as possible.

By morning Edmund was worse: he complained of a sore throat, vomiting and diarrhoea. Dr Elwell was called again, and at about noon his partner, Dr John Binning, came to examine the patient. Again there was no obvious diagnosis. Edmund Duff had a stomach upset, that much was clear, but it seemed nothing out of the ordinary. Dr Binning prescribed calomel and took his leave, confident that Edmund's discomfort would soon pass.

In the afternoon the continuing vomiting and diarrhoea were accompanied by severe abdominal pains, and by the time Dr Elwell called back to see his patient later in the afternoon, Edmund was in a seriously weakened state. The doctor was still at a loss to explain the cause of these symptoms, other than assuming that Edmund must have eaten something that disagreed with him. Dr Binning took his turn to visit Edmund in the early evening and saw a marked deterioration in his condition. The stomach cramps were now agonizing and Edmund was too light-headed to stand unaided. He lay in his bed shivering in a cold sweat. For the first time, Dr Binning considered the possibility that the condition might be fatal, and telephoned Dr Elwell to communicate his concerns. When Grace called the surgery again that night to tell them that Edmund had difficulty in breathing, both doctors attended him. They administered whatever they could to ease his pain but shortly after eleven o'clock Edmund Duff died, leaving a near-hysterical widow and an unanswered mystery.

As neither of the doctors could satisfactorily explain Edmund's death, it was left to a post-mortem and inquest to find the answers. Grace and the children had eaten the same food as Edmund, albeit at a different time, and they were all quite well. The only difference was that Edmund had drunk a small tot of whisky on the journey home and some beer with his meal. Edmund had started to feel unwell before he arrived home, which suggested that if food had caused his sickness, it must have been ingested prior to his return. Edmund's host on the fishing trip in

Hampshire, Harold Edwardes, confirmed that no one from his household had suffered from food poisoning. The pathology laboratory found no signs of food poisoning in Edmund's body and the only toxic substances found could be accounted for by the medication administered by the doctors. It was a puzzle. One suggestion was that the sickness might have been brought on by sunstroke during his fishing trip and his death caused by subsequent heart failure. It must, then, have been death from natural causes, concluded the Coroner's Court.

At the age of forty Vera Sidney lived an active, if quiet, life with her mother, Violet. She still had most of her inheritance of £5,000, and this gave her the freedom to work at her job as a masseuse with a few select clients and to spend the rest of her time as she chose. She enjoyed bridge and brisk walks and was a member of Croham Hurst Golf Club. She began feeling unwell in January 1929. To start with it was just a general sense of fatigue, explained, she felt, by recent sleeplessness. Never one to wallow in self-pity, she tried to overlook this weariness and get on with her life. Then she started to feel nauseous for no obvious reason. On Sunday, 10 February she felt so unwell that she didn't leave the house at all. Her sister Grace visited her, and seemed very concerned. The next day Vera awoke with a determination to pull herself together, and went for a long walk in the morning and played bridge in the afternoon. That evening she dined with her mother as usual, eating soup that the maid had prepared using a soup powder and fresh vegetables. This was followed by fish and potatoes, then a pudding. Vera was the only one at the dinner table to eat the soup; Violet never did. However, their maid, Mrs Kathleen Noakes, had tasted a small quantity of it in the kitchen and had given some to the cat. That night Vera, Mrs Noakes and the cat were all sick.

On Wednesday, 13 February Vera was slightly better. She ran some errands in the morning and returned to have lunch at home with her mother and her Aunt Gwen. Grace had collected Gwen from South Croydon railway station, but she was unable to stay for lunch herself because of the children. Mrs Noakes had prepared another soup, this time with veal and vegetables, and she used the same soup powder as before. Vera and Gwen had the soup, although Gwen left most of hers, and almost as soon as the meal was over both women were sick. Vera was convinced it was the soup that had caused them to be ill, and questioned the maid about it. All the utensils had been scrupulously cleaned, Mrs Noakes assured her, and although the veal had been left over from another meal, she was sure there was nothing wrong with it. The only ingredient that had been in both soups was the soup powder.

That evening Vera became significantly worse, with severe pains in her stomach and now in her legs. Grace was shocked by her sister's condition and called Dr Elwell, who visited her at about nine o'clock. He stayed with her for three hours, returning at one in the morning to give her morphine to ease her pain. The following day, Thursday, Dr Elwell attended her again, staying for most of the day. He consulted with Dr Binning and they decided to seek the advice of a specialist, Dr Charles Bolton, who examined Vera and diagnosed gastro-intestinal influenza. Vera was in agony. Dr Binning stayed with her while Dr Elwell went to fetch a nurse, but at 12.20 in the morning of Friday, 15 February 1929 Vera died.

Because of Dr Bolton's confident diagnosis, Dr Binning and Dr Elwell saw nothing suspicious in Vera's death and attributed it to natural causes.

To say that the loss of her daughter upset Violet is an understatement. Vera had been her close companion and her death had been sudden. Tom and Grace were extremely concerned at the extent of their mother's distress and they each visited her every day after Vera's death. Dr Elwell, too, was a regular visitor, prescribing the tonics Metatone and Phylosan to help Violet through her grief.

On the morning of Tuesday, 5 March Grace visited her mother, as did Dr Elwell. Violet ate her lunch alone, cooked and served by Mrs Noakes, but afterwards she felt rather sick. When Grace came back to see her mother in the early afternoon she was shocked to see her looking so pale. Violet told her she thought she had been poisoned, and that her last dose of Metatone had tasted odd. Grace gave her salt water and called the surgery. It was Dr Binning who came. He listened to Violet's theory about the Metatone and examined the bottle to see if it might have been contaminated. He found gritty sediment in the bottom of the bottle and telephoned the chemist who had dispensed the medicine to enquire whether there might be anything in the tonic that could explain Violet's symptoms. It contained a small dose of strychnine, the chemist confirmed, but so small that it could not possibly have any adverse effect.

Tom arrived later in the afternoon, when his mother became considerably worse. She was suffering from both vomiting and diarrhoea and appeared to be on the point of collapse. Dr Elwell sought the opinion of a specialist, Dr Poynton, who suggested it might be either food poisoning or metal poisoning. With Grace, Tom, Dr Binning and Dr Elwell at her bedside, Violet died that evening.

The police became involved at this point. Although Violet's

The exhumation of the bodies. Hulton Picture Library

death was difficult to explain, her burial went ahead and she was laid next to Vera at the Queen's Road Cemetery. But she was not to rest for long. The police investigation was intensifying and on 22 March the exhumations began.

The inquests into the deaths of Edmund Duff, Vera Sidney and Violet Sidney were heard separately, taking up an astonishing twenty-six sessions at the Coroner's Court. No one was ever brought to trial on a charge of murder, even though the chances of three members of one family dying of accidental poisoning in separate incidents seem impossibly unlikely.

Investigations showed that all three died of arsenic poisoning. In the second autopsy carried out on Edmund Duff, arsenic was found throughout his body and they concluded that he must have ingested a considerable amount. It was embarrassing for the doctors to have to make such a volte-face after stating so categorically that there was no sign of poisoning in the first post-mortem. Their explanation was that they had originally tested 'the only organ' not to contain arsenic, and therefore did not look further. Their incompetence had been exposed. The next problem was to discover how the arsenic had been ingested. It was thought to have been administered to Edmund either in the beer he had with his last meal, or in a flask of whisky he took with him on his fishing trip. With Vera the soup was the obvious vehicle for the poison, since other people had been affected by it too. Traces of arsenic were found in Violet's bottle of Metatone and in the glass she used for her medicine. In each case only the victims were likely to have consumed the poisoned food or drink: Edmund's beer and whisky were reserved for him alone, only Vera regularly ate soup at mealtimes, and Violet's medicine was exclusively hers. Two questions remained: who had placed the poison in such specifically targeted food and drink, and why?

There were a number of suspects, none of whom had an obvious motive, but who may have had the opportunity to administer the arsenic. They included Grace, Tom, the doctors and Mrs Noakes, and it was even suggested that Violet might have murdered Edmund and Vera before killing herself. Theories abounded.

The least likely suspect is Mrs Noakes: she had absolutely no motive and no access to Edmund Duff's beer or whisky. Although Violet was strict with her, there seems to have been no ill feeling between Mrs Noakes and her mistress. There is also the fact that she drank some of the first batch of soup – she was hardly likely to poison herself.

Both of the doctors had access to all three victims, and it is an interesting point that all three normally healthy victims had felt generally unwell immediately prior to the poisonings. And there was a possible motive for Dr Elwell to want Edmund Duff out of the way, if contemporary rumours were to be believed. It was said that Dr Elwell had romantic feelings for Grace, and certainly following Edmund's death their relationship appeared to be more than that of doctor and patient; they were unusually close. Many people expected Grace to marry Dr Elwell and the idea was said to be looked on favourably by both Tom and Violet. It came to nothing, however, so it is hard to say how much truth there was in the rumour and how much it was mere conjecture. But even if local gossip were true, it would not provide an explanation for the deaths of Vera and Violet.

That Violet had murdered Edmund and Vera before committing suicide also seems an unlikely theory. She may have had a strong dislike of Edmund Duff, but she took care to hide it beneath a civil exterior, and there is no reason to believe her capable of murdering him. It is hard to believe that she would poison the daughter she was so very close to – it was obvious to everyone that Vera was the favoured child. And if Violet had wanted to commit suicide, she would surely have chosen a less painful method, especially after having witnessed Vera's agonizing death. This theory was treated with derision by the surviving members of the family.

Tom remains a slightly elusive character. He was struggling to support his family as an entertainer, and his wife wanted to set up home in the United States. Greed is a possible motive for Tom killing his sister and mother, but the same applies to Grace. Both were short of funds, and both inherited thousands of pounds from the wills: Vera had left £5,500 and Violet's estate exceeded £11,000. However, apart from having a passing dislike of his brother-in-law, there was no obvious reason for Tom to kill Edmund. Tom, though, was a suspect in the eyes of the police and a recent television programme about the murders pointed the finger of blame directly at him.

Then there was Grace. She was seen by many, both at the time and since, as the prime suspect. She had open access to all three victims, and stood to gain financially from all three deaths, though with Edmund it was more a case of stemming the flow of her husband's expenditure rather than a positive inheritance. Was her marriage as happy as it seemed, and was she perhaps influenced by Dr Elwell's feelings for her? If Grace was guilty, she put up a stunning performance as the grieving widow and the distraught daughter and sister.

It is, of course, a possibility that there was more than one murderer. Grace and Dr Elwell would have made an efficient team, for example. It has also been suggested that Violet might have killed Edmund, provoking Grace to retaliate by killing Violet's favourite daughter before murdering Violet herself. There is ample opportunity to speculate.

What we do know is that the murderer was intimately acquainted with the victims, knowing the patterns of their lives well enough to target the poison with maximum accuracy. Tins of weedkiller containing arsenic were found in the garden sheds of all three households; the method, then, was readily available to all the suspects. But the question of who committed the Birdhurst Rise murders remains a mystery to this day. In the words of Tom's wife, Margaret: 'There are several people who may have committed the crimes. Who can say who did it?'

CHAPTER 2

I Die For Love:
Eliza Osborne, 1877

He crawled to her side and kissed her three or four times.

The battle against poverty was one that Caleb Smith appeared to be losing. Following the death of his wife at the end of 1875, he struggled to keep his family fed and housed, moving from place to place with three of his four children. His eldest daughter, aged sixteen, was in service. Early in the spring of 1877 he settled into rooms at number 2, Collier's Yard, South End, Croydon, a poor part of town then renowned for its squalor. With them lived Eliza Osborne. She had known Caleb during his wife's lifetime and had moved in with him

South End, Croydon. Croydon Local Studies Library

South End, Croydon. Croydon Local Studies Library

and his family just one short month after his wife's death. Although this was looked on as a scandal in itself, the situation was made worse by the fact that Eliza Osborne had a husband still living. The *Croydon Advertiser* reported that 'the morality exhibited by persons of this class is not always of the strictest kind. In the case of Osborne the marriage-tie appears to have been lightly regarded.' Eliza's husband was a hawker by profession and all the evidence suggests that he was still in love with her. He wrote an open and touching letter to their fourteen-year-old son begging him to ask his mother to return to him. He promised to buy her a new 'frock and shawl' and said that he would wait for them both at Bishop Stortford station. Eliza went with her son to East Croydon station, saw him onto the train, then left on her own to return to Caleb Smith at Collier's Yard.

Caleb was painfully aware of how little he could offer Eliza. Now aged thirty-eight, just two years older than the woman he loved, he took a job at the Croydon Gas Works in order to provide for his family. But we know from newspaper reports that their living conditions were far from easy. The *Croydon Advertiser* wrote that 'Smith's place of residence was a four-roomed cottage, the interior of which exhibits evidence of the direst poverty.' The building itself was dilapidated and their few rooms sparsely furnished. There was nothing but a table and a few hard chairs in the living room and the children slept on mattresses on the floor of one of the upstairs rooms. 'Miserable' was a word used by more than one reporter. Nevertheless Caleb and Eliza lived relatively quietly with the children and, according to neighbours, behaved well.

Caleb later told the police that trouble started between them when friends of Eliza decided that she could do better than live with a man who provided so poorly. Jane and Charlie Warner tried to convince Eliza that she should move her affections elsewhere, and introduced her to a man who worked as a gardener and earned a much better wage. It was the cause of a series of arguments between Caleb and Eliza, and both jealousy and the fear of losing the partner he cared for so very much drove him to despair. At the end of March, Eliza moved away from Collier's Yard and spent two weeks living with the Warners. Caleb was fearful that they would persuade her away from him for ever, but she did return, on Sunday, 8 April, one week before her murder.

On the evening of Saturday, 14 April Caleb and Eliza took

Britannia *public house.* Croydon Local Studies Library

Annie, Caleb's daughter, who was ten years old and the eldest of those children still living at Collier's Yard, into the town centre. They visited several public houses during the course of the evening, including the *Britannia* and the *Royal Oak*. Annie left them fairly early in the evening, at about eight o'clock, and returned home to the younger children while Caleb and Eliza continued drinking. They met Jane Warner, Eliza's interfering friend, in the *Britannia*, and from there the arguments started, fuelled by jealousy and alcohol.

Annie recalled that her father and Eliza returned home shortly after eleven o'clock. They brought more beer home with them and invited Katharine Cronin, who lived nearby, to drink it with them. But they were unable to stop arguing, even in the company of their neighbour, and at one point Eliza slapped Caleb's face. Katharine noted that he did nothing whatsoever in retaliation. And so, although angry words had been spoken, there was nothing to suggest that the night would turn to serious violence.

Katharine Cronin went back to her rooms, leaving Annie still up with her father and Eliza. Perhaps one of the saddest aspects of this case is that the ten-year-old girl was present to witness all the scenes that followed.

Royal Oak *public house.* Croydon Local Studies Library

Southbridge Road. Croydon Local Studies Library

Whether Eliza was seriously considering the possibility of leaving Caleb, or whether it was the drink talking we shall never know. But as the argument went into the early hours of Sunday morning Caleb asked Eliza to kiss him, and this she did. He then walked to the fire, and without either Annie or Eliza seeing, picked up the cut-throat razor that lay on the mantelpiece. Calmly he returned to Eliza, knelt down by her chair and slit her throat. Annie screamed. Eliza slumped to the floor and the child realized in that moment what her father meant to do next. As he took the razor to his own throat she shouted, 'Father, pray father, don't do it!' But it was too late.

Their nearest neighbour, Hannah Scott, heard Annie's screams, and came out immediately to find out what was happening. The door was unlocked and she walked in to a scene that defied belief. Eliza was lying on her side, her face and throat covered in blood, as was the floor around her head. She appeared lifeless. Caleb lay not far from her, and though alive, he was in a poor state. In shock, Hannah ran outside screaming for help. She found Police Sergeant Ashley in Southbridge Road and they returned together to Collier's Yard.

Believing himself to be on the point of death, Caleb gave the police officer the only explanation he could: 'I die for love,' he said, quite simply. He was bleeding profusely from the self-inflicted wound and PS Ashley realized he would need urgent medical treatment. Arrangements were made to take him by cab

Croydon General Hospital c.1894. Croydon Local Studies Library

to Croydon General Hospital, and at this Caleb became agitated once more, begging to be allowed to kiss Eliza before they took him away. Without waiting for an answer he crawled to her side and kissed her three or four times.

Eliza's body was taken to the Infirmary at Duppas Hill, and Caleb's three young children went to the Croydon Union Workhouse, where, according to the newspapers at least, they were well looked after. And Caleb, who had just lost what little he had in life, was left in hospital to recover and grieve. And the grief proved to be more than he could bear.

On 20 April, less than a week after Eliza's death, he made another, quite desperate, attempt to take his own life. He was kept under constant police guard in the hospital, but as he recovered from the wound to his throat he was able to do more for himself. Early on the Friday morning he asked for water, soap and a towel so that he could wash himself. PC Counihan stood a few feet from him. Caleb moved to the fire to warm himself after he had washed, rubbed his hands together and made idle remarks about how cold the morning was. The window to his second-floor room was just three feet away from him, and the constable stood to his other side. With the police officer's guard momentarily relaxed, Caleb took his chance and ran at the window, diving head first through it. PC Counihan's response was swift, and he managed to catch him by one leg, leaving him dangling outside the window twelve feet above the ground. But Caleb was determined to fall

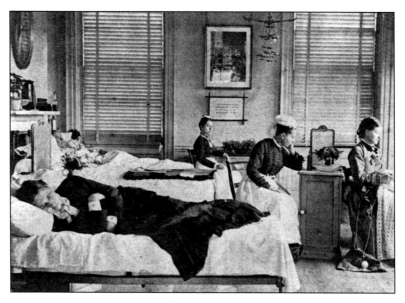

Inside the Infirmary, Duppas Hill. Croydon Local Studies Library

and struggled until the officer was no longer able to hold on to him. He was plainly hoping to end his life but gained nothing more than a fractured hip and a much stricter police guard.

Caleb Smith appeared at the Croydon Assizes in July 1877, charged with the wilful murder of Eliza Osborne. He expressed no remorse for the crime, only for the fact that he had been unable to kill himself too. While at the hospital he had confided to his police guard that he had been watching her behaviour closely and contemplating the act for at least a month before the crime was committed. But the circumstances of the murder were unusual, and the judge was aware that the jury's sympathies would be engaged in Caleb's favour, especially following the tearful evidence given by his daughter Annie. Mr Justice Grove warned the jury not to be 'actuated by feelings of sympathy', but to do their duty, however painful that might be, with the broader interests of the public in mind. Despite slight applause in the courtroom when Caleb's counsel suggested that the charge be reduced to manslaughter on the grounds of provocation, the jury found him guilty of murder. Before donning the black cap to pass sentence of death, the judge addressed Caleb directly:

I may say the crime you have committed is not so horrible to the human mind as that in which there is a murder committed from baser motives, but still the law regards them as the same. A man is

Croydon Union Workhouse. Croydon Local Studies Library

not allowed, because he has a strong and devoted attachment to a woman, to take away her life; nor indeed may a man take away his own life.

As the death sentence was passed on him, Caleb Smith showed no emotion. He left the court remarking to one of the warders that, in all, his trial had been fair, and that the judge had summed up the case to the jury well. He was a man resigned to his fate.

Before his execution he was allowed to see all four of his children. The *Croydon Advertiser* reported that 'the younger children clung to their father, and it was with difficulty they were removed from the cell.' From the close of his trial to the day of his execution Caleb was kept under strict guard, ironically because of fears of another suicide attempt. His behaviour during this time, however, was said to be exemplary, his days being spent in reading the Bible, writing letters to his family and in earnest discussion with the prison chaplain.

On Tuesday, 14 August 1877 Caleb went to his execution within the walls of the Surrey County Prison. His executioner, a man by the name of Marwood, decided that given Smith's height of 5 feet 8 inches, a drop of 6 to 7 feet would be sufficient to kill him. Caleb's last words were to express a determination to die for

Eliza 'like a man'. The *Croydon Advertiser* reported his final moments in some detail:

> *The convict emerged from his cell a few minutes before the appointed hour for his execution, and was pinioned in the corridor leading to the yard. He was pale and haggard and submitted very quietly to the operation. Having taken his place on the spot, where he was to expiate his crime, a cap was drawn over the doomed man's face, the fatal noose was adjusted, the bolt was withdrawn, and the body fell with a heavy thud. There were a few convulsive movements for a minute or so, and then all was over.*

CHAPTER 3

No Clues, No Motive:
Miles Vallint, 1959

After kissing his mother goodbye he promised to be back by 4.30.

Detective Superintendent Albert Denton headed the murder inquiry, and it was his duty to present the findings of the police investigation to the inquest held at Croydon Town Hall. There was very little he could say. 'There was no motive,' he reported, 'and no clues. We have not even found the instrument which, apparently, caused the death of this boy.' He described the killing as a 'very evil act', and reassured the inquest jury that 'we have used the whole of our resources to try to find the person responsible.' The jury had no choice but to return a verdict of murder by person or persons unknown.

Eleven-year-old Miles Vallint had lived with his family in Farnley Road, South Norwood. He was particularly excited on Thursday, 27 August 1959 because he was going into Croydon to choose the bicycle his father had promised to buy him for his birthday. In three weeks' time he would be twelve. He set off at half past one, wearing his Lone Ranger shirt, and, after kissing his mother goodbye, promised to be back by 4.30. He had just 10d. in his pocket for his bus fare there and back.

It was not the first time Miles had gone into Croydon town centre on his own. He was used to travelling there on the bus to buy pens, pencils and the other small items he needed for school. But it turned out to be his last.

Miles was a pupil at St Joseph's College, Beulah Hill, Upper Norwood. He took his school work seriously, and was generally thought to be a good student. He loved football, cricket and most other sports, though he was especially fond of swimming. He was also a member of the 58th Croydon Scout Troop.

Miles was remembered as a quiet, shy boy, lightly built for his age, and certainly not one to associate with 'the rough lads'.

Detective Superintendent A Denton.
Croydon Advertiser

Miles Vallint. Croydon Times courtesy of the *Croydon Advertiser*

He was very close to his family, and spent a lot of his time during the school holidays playing with his cousins. He had recently returned from a school trip to Spain, and had spent his pocket money on small presents for them – all thirteen of them! In fact the whole family was close-knit. His father, Frank, described by those who knew him as 'a distinguished-looking man', came from India, and Miles himself had been born in Calcutta. His mother was English, and on the day he set out for Croydon to look for his bicycle, she walked him to the

St Joseph's College. Croydon Local Studies Library

The boys of St Joseph's College. Croydon Local Studies Library

corner of the road to see him safely off. She had often reminded him not to talk to strangers.

When he didn't come home at 4.30 as promised, his family thought he must have met up with one of his cousins. It was unlike Miles not to do as he was told, but it was the most obvious explanation. As the time rolled by their anxieties increased and one of his uncles went into Croydon to look for him. By nine o'clock in the evening they had confronted their fears and reported him to the police as missing. They then faced a long night waiting for news and hoping for a miracle.

Forty-four-year-old Robert Davis was sleeping rough. He had arrived at the waste ground in Tavistock Road shortly before eleven o'clock that evening and busied himself placing sheets of corrugated iron against the wall to provide some sort of shelter for the night. The land had formed part of the garden of the recently demolished vicarage, and rubble was strewn everywhere. He heard nothing and saw nothing until he woke just before seven the following morning. He got up, stretched and had his first cigarette of the day. Then he noticed a pair of feet hanging over the mattress on the rubbish heap on the far side of the site. They looked like the feet of a young boy. Robert Davis walked quietly towards the boy thinking he might still be asleep, but then he got close enough to see properly. When he realized that the boy was not sleeping at all he went straight to the police.

David Haler, the pathologist who examined Miles's body, expressed the opinion that Miles had not been killed at the spot where he was found; there was evidence that his body had lain for some time in a completely different position. He had been strangled. But the injury was decidedly unusual – there were no marks at the sides or back of the neck, only a very deep indentation at the front. 'There was no knot mark,' Mr Haler explained at the inquest, 'as there would have been if the ligature was tied round the neck. It was a very violent injury, and had burned the skin by the pressure of the application.' Such an injury is extremely difficult to explain, given that there were no other marks on the neck.

Miles's body had been found at about seven o'clock in the morning. By nine o'clock Mrs Vallint was walking from shop to shop in Croydon, bearing both a photograph of her son and a fierce determination to track his last movements. The police were making house-to-house inquiries, and as the day wore on the search broadened to cover as much ground as possible. Checks were made on any patients who had recently left mental institutions; schoolchildren were questioned; neighbours in the Tavistock Road area, where Miles was found, were interviewed one by one; police cars with loudspeakers drove up and down North End prompting shoppers to report anything suspicious that might relate to the murder; appeals were made to cinemagoers by

The funeral wreath made for Miles in the shape of a bicycle. Croydon Times *courtesy of the* Croydon Advertiser

means of photographs flashed onto the theatre screen. No new details surfaced.

The only real information came from the bicycle shops, and from this the police did trace Miles's movements up to the middle of the afternoon on Thursday, 27 August. He had been to a shop in London Road, Croydon, owned by Mr Stanley Batts, and spent about twenty minutes looking at the bicycles there. This was shortly after two o'clock. He moved on to a cycle shop in Whitehorse Road, where he was given a handful of catalogues by Mrs Susan Larkin, then on to yet another in London Road, where he stayed until about 3.30. He was remembered there because he had been so polite.

The only other possible sighting of Miles came slightly later, at approximately four o'clock. Mrs Ellen Davidson felt she recognized Miles from photographs circulated by police as being the young boy who came into her hardware shop to buy a length of washing line. The *Norwood News* reported:

> *While dealing with another customer she was aware of a man in the doorway and Miles asking him which rope he should take. The one he chose cost 4s. 11d. 'He was just a very untidy, unkempt sort of man. Not a tramp, just rough,' she said. She also said there was a small boy with Miles.*

Whether this was a correct identification of Miles or not was never verified. Despite repeated appeals to members of the public who might recognize the description of the man, or the little boy with him, nothing new came to light. The Vallint family was never to discover the full truth about their son's death. No one was ever brought to justice. But they had, at least, recovered his body, and they were able to bid him a final farewell.

Miles was buried on Wednesday, 2 September 1959. Hundreds of boys from his school turned up to pay their last respects, and his coffin was carried into the church by four of the sixth-formers. Members of the 58th Croydon Scout Troop formed a guard of honour. Miles did eventually get his bicycle, but it was not in the way that either he or his parents had planned. It came in the form of a wreath made of yellow and bronze chrysanthemums, and was carried next to his coffin at the funeral.

CHAPTER 4

Kenley Stud Farm Mystery:
Gordon Eric Gordon-Tombe, 1922

Then his mother had a dream . . .

The writer Dennis Wheatley published a series of novels based on the occult, but nothing in his books could have been stranger than the true-life story of two of his friends, Gordon Eric Gordon-Tombe and Ernest 'Bill' Dyer. He was particularly close to Gordon-Tombe, referring to him in his autobiography as 'the most intimate of all my friends' and claiming that 'I owed more to him than to any other person in my life.' Indeed, his memoirs are dedicated to his father, his grandfathers and Gordon Eric Gordon-Tombe, 'who between them', says Wheatley, 'made me what I am.' He even based one of his fictional characters, Gregory Sallust, on Gordon-Tombe.

The real-life story ended in the death of both friends, one of them murdered, and although Wheatley gives the murder little more than a cursory mention in his autobiography, a series of private papers sold at auction in 1985 indicate that his interest went far deeper. *The Times* reported:

> *Wheatley had an obsession with the murder and a close involvement with the strange circumstances of the death. . . . He had also kept a meticulous library of letters and press cuttings relating to the murder case. The contrast between what Wheatley recorded in his official biography and what is contained in these papers is startling. Had they been available at the time, he would have been a prime suspect.*

The friendship began back in the First World War when Wheatley and Gordon-Tombe were fighting on the Western Front. It was an experience that left physical and mental scars on both men, Wheatley surviving a gas attack and Gordon-Tombe being buried alive when a shell exploded close to him. The third friend, Bill Dyer, was a veteran of both Gallipoli and Passchendaele. As for so many others, these were events that had a profound influence on their attitudes to life thereafter, keeping them on the periphery of mainstream society. Gordon-Tombe was a self-confessed hedonist and, according to Dennis Wheatley, 'a crook of the first order'. In this he was well-partnered by Dyer, an Australian who was a great gambler and risk-taker.

Hayes Lane, Kenley and Welcomes Farm. Croydon Local Studies Library

Gordon-Tombe and Dyer set up several ventures together, the last of which was a stud farm in Hayes Lane, Kenley, called The Welcomes. It was an enormous sixteen-bedroomed house set in five acres of land, and its hilltop location afforded it spectacular views over the surrounding countryside. But they had no intention of breeding horses – it was apparently an insurance scam intended to make their fortune. Gordon-Tombe fronted the capital for the stud farm, but Dyer lived there with his family. Wheatley recalls a day in April 1922 when Gordon-Tombe invited him to dine – but it was not a straightforward invitation. Gordon-Tombe needed an alibi for the evening, he said, and so they would be in the company of two young ladies, one of whom had previously been a mistress of Wheatley's. Gordon-Tombe warned Wheatley that he might be late, but that if questions were later asked, they might say that they had all four been together all evening. Out of friendship Wheatley agreed. Gordon-Tombe did arrive late, at about midnight in fact, wearing white tie, tails and a top hat so that anyone seeing him would assume he had been attending the formal dance that was being held locally that night. What he and Dyer had actually been doing required less formal attire; he had, according to Wheatley, been burning down the house on The Welcomes estate so that they could make an insurance claim against the property. They left the outbuildings untouched. He said they had placed combustible material beneath the floors of the house, set fire to it, and then,

Milking time at the Welcomes Farm. Croydon Local Studies Library

while Gordon-Tombe kept his appointment with Dennis Wheatley and the young ladies, Bill Dyer had headed for Brighton.

The risk did not pay off. The insurance company refused to pay out and Gordon Eric Gordon-Tombe went to The Welcomes a few weeks later to discover what had gone wrong. He was never seen by friends or family again.

An inquiry into his disappearance began. Wheatley was asked by Gordon-Tombe's girlfriend to hire a private detective to track him down, but the detective agency unsettled Wheatley with its line of questioning. In his autobiography he says the head of the agency 'asked me many questions that I dared not answer truthfully because I did know in a general way about Gordon Eric's criminal activities in the past and feared to compromise him.'

There seemed to be no trace of Gordon Eric Gordon-Tombe. Wheatley was anxious to distance himself from any police investigation into the affair. He was about to marry a wealthy heiress and wanted no scandal to spoil his wedding plans. If the true extent of his dealings with Gordon-Tombe, and his knowledge of the allegedly fraudulent activities of Gordon-Tombe and Dyer became known, he might have been dragged in more deeply than he wished. For his relationship with Gordon-Tombe did not bear

Main yard at the Welcomes after the fire. Croydon Local Studies Library

close scrutiny. *The Times* reported, in an article written in 1996, that the men shared sexual partners, in threesomes and sometimes foursomes, and that their appreciation of young men was another common interest.

In his official biography Wheatley admits to being distressed by Gordon-Tombe's disappearance, but says that he was thankfully distracted by his wedding preparations. This may be something of a misleading statement. In his private papers he reveals he was extremely worried for his close friend, to such an extent that no imminent marriage celebration could offer distraction. His official version was that he had no idea what had happened to Gordon-Tombe, but his unpublished memoirs offer a different view. *The Times* quotes from his papers:

> *In my mind I condemned Bill* [Dyer] . . . *There's only one man who could surely make me feel afraid and that's Bill. Those deep black cruel eyes of his make me shudder. He'd be a murderous fellow to get up against.*

But Dyer was covering the tracks. He told friends that he had received a telegram from Gordon-Tombe saying that he needed to be out of the country for a week or so. This was, in some ways, credible. Gordon-Tombe's close friends knew him to be involved in shady affairs that might require his sudden absence. But as the days moved into weeks and the weeks into months, everyone knew that something was seriously amiss. This fear was supported by the detective agency's discovery that the telegram, supposedly sent by Gordon-Tombe, was false.

'I would like to have seen Dyer hanged,' said Wheatley in his published autobiography, 'but Fate had already caught up with him in a curious way.' On 23 November 1922, seven months after the disappearance of his friend and business partner, Dyer was found in the Bath Hotel in Scarborough. Financially he was in serious trouble and had turned to fraud yet again to raise funds. Using the name James Vincent Fitzsimmons, he had placed an advertisement in a local Scarborough newspaper that was essentially a confidence trick aimed at separating ex-servicemen from their pensions. The police saw the advertisement and went to question Dyer. He was finishing his lunch at the hotel when they arrived and initially he answered their questions. They were not satisfied with his answers, however, and demanded both proof of his identity and permission to search through his belongings. 'There's nothing to stop you seeing them,' Dyer said. 'Let's go upstairs.' The *Croydon Times* takes up the story:

> *When they got up one flight witness* [Detective Inspector Abbott] *noticed a movement of Dyer's arm, and he and another officer rushed on him, and it was noticed Dyer had a revolver. They all struggled and fell on the floor. Then there was a report, and witness at first thought it was a bluff, but on examining Dyer found that he was dead, having died instantaneously.*

He was killed by his own hand, maybe accidentally, although some have suggested suicide.

When the police later searched his room they found Gordon Eric Gordon-Tombe's passport, several personal items such as a hairbrush and address book marked with the initials G.E.G.T. and a passbook for a bank account in the same name. The account had been emptied of funds, using forged documents in both the London and Paris branches of the bank. Bill Dyer was only twenty-nine years old and had spent most of his adult life concocting money-making schemes of one sort or another. It was all to no avail – he died a pauper and was given a pauper's funeral.

But now the mystery of Gordon-Tombe's disappearance was looking very sinister, and the only person who might have shed light on it was dead himself.

The mystery was finally solved in such as a bizarre fashion that if it appeared on

Dream led police
to body in
cesspool

Croydon Advertiser

the pages of a novel it would be dismissed as incredible. Gordon-Tombe's parents were not willing to give up the search for their son, even if his friends had given up hope. They were convinced, for some reason they could not explain, that he was dead and not simply missing. The last letter they had received from their son had been sent on 18 April 1922. By mid-June they were extremely worried; it was not like him to allow quite so much time to elapse without contacting them, regardless of his circumstances. 'I knew it was impossible for my son, if he was alive, not to write to me. He was a very affectionate lad,' said Mrs Gordon-Tombe. His father, the Reverend George Gordon-Tombe, wrote to an address in Jermyn Street, a bureau that his son often used for mail. The bureau had seen and heard nothing from him since 20 April. The Reverend and Mrs Gordon-Tombe reported him missing to Scotland Yard, and placed advertisements in both the local and national press. For months they heard nothing.

Then his mother had a dream. In the dream she saw her son's body shut up or locked up at the bottom of a well, near a burnt-out building. He was calling out to her to let him out. The dream was vivid, so vivid that the Reverend and Mrs Gordon-Tombe went back to the police and urged them to search the premises at The Welcomes more thoroughly. They agreed to do this and made enquiries of Mr John Hales, who used to work as a groom at The Welcomes, asking him if he knew of any wells on the premises. There were no wells that he knew of, Mr Hales told them, but the stud farm did have a number of disused cesspits. The search began. The first two were empty, but the third and largest was filled with rubble and covered at the top by a large stone slab. The police worked to clear the in-fill and on the afternoon of 12 September 1923, found a body. It looked as though it had been thrown in head first, as the head was lower than the rest of the body, jammed into the concrete and rubble; one arm was doubled underneath the body and the other was outstretched. Mr Hales pointed out that no one could have fallen down that cesspit accidentally. The body was in an advanced state of decay – it had been almost one year and five months since Gordon-Tombe's disappearance, but it took just one glance for Mr Hales to work out who it was:

The body when I saw it was dressed as I had seen Mr Tombe, in a brown reefer suit. He was wearing a black woollen scarf. I was able at once to recognize it as that of Mr Tombe by the boots, as he always walked inside his heels . . . also by the gold tooth in the left upper jaw, which I used to notice when Mr Tombe smiled.

The identification was backed up by the Reverend Gordon-Tombe. He was able to identify a number of articles belonging to his son: a silk pocket handkerchief, the brown suit, the overcoat and the wristwatch. The *Croydon Advertiser* reported that:

> *Following the discovery the remains were placed in a sack and taken to Bandon Hill Cemetery in a farmer's cart. They were minutely examined by Dr Stanley Brook, of Lister House, Godstone Road, Purley, the Divisional Surgeon.*

What he found was that Gordon-Tombe's death could not possibly have been suicide and was extremely unlikely to have been an accident. The Divisional Surgeon was convinced he was looking at a murder victim. Four pellets were removed from the skull, the entry wounds being just behind the victim's right ear. The skull itself was fractured, although that most probably occurred as the body was thrown into the cesspit. Dr Brook felt that the shots had been fired from behind and at very close range, possibly as close as three feet.

At the inquest, Bill Dyer's wife gave a very interesting account of one of her last evenings at The Welcomes. Bill Dyer had been away for a week or two, and she was unaware that he had returned home. The *Croydon Times* took up her story:

> *At eleven o'clock one night she heard a noise as if someone was throwing stones down a drain. She was then in the cottage, and got the dog. The dog took her across to a cowshed facing the stables, and here she saw her husband standing. She said, 'What are you doing here?' and he replied that owing to the state of his credit he did not want to be seen in daylight. He was in a state of agitation in the house. . . . She had heard her husband threaten what he would do to Tombe if he met him.*

The inquest jury returned a verdict of wilful murder against Dyer, and since Gordon-Tombe had not been seen since 20 April, estimated the date of his death to be 21 April 1922. In accordance with his parents' wishes, the funeral of Gordon Eric Gordon-Tombe was both simple and quiet, a stark contrast to his rich and colourful life, the complexities of which will remain as much a mystery as his death.

CHAPTER 5

Murder Most Mysterious:
James Joseph Tyrrell, 1959

I do forgive him and I bear him no malice.

A murder must be classified as mysterious if even the murderer has no understanding of his motive for having committed the crime. Strange as it may seem, such was the case of William John Storie, a supervisor at the Wallington Telephone Exchange. At the Magistrates' hearing of the case, Mr A G Flavell, acting for the prosecution, summed up in these words: 'There must have been a reason for the attack, but if there was one it remains a mystery.'

On the morning of 12 March 1959, William Storie went to the home of James Tyrrell, known to his friends as 'Jimmy'. Jimmy, a telephone operator at the Croydon Exchange, acted as collector for the Mutual Aid Fund Insurance Society at the Croydon branch. The fund worked quite simply – when a member died every other member paid sixpence and this sum was given to the bereaved family. However, William Storie, who until recently had also worked at the Croydon Exchange, hadn't paid anything for over two years. Instead, Jimmy Tyrrell had paid the subscriptions on Storie's behalf and if ever he asked for the money, Storie would brush it off with, 'See you later on,' until the outstanding amount built up to 27 shillings. It was a significant sum of money for a working man in 1959, but Tyrrell didn't seem to have been unduly concerned. In fact he claimed that he kept forgetting to ask Storie for the money. So if William Storie was not being pressed for the money, it was probably not a motive for trying to kill Tyrrell.

The first time William Storie called at the Tyrrell's house, Jimmy was still asleep and James Tyrrell senior answered the door. Storie didn't stop, but returned later that day at about half past three. This time Jimmy was up and invited William Storie into the back garden. There they chatted, about the Mutual Aid Fund among other things. In Storie's words, 'Jimmy was a bit of a muddler as far as book-keeping was concerned,' and Storie wanted to straighten out how he was going to repay his outstanding contributions now that he had moved to the Wallington Exchange. Jimmy seemed relaxed about the whole thing. It was arranged that Storie would make his back payments to the Wallington collector, and Jimmy would collect the money from his colleague.

William Storie was on the night shift at the exchange in Wallington, and started work at seven o'clock that same evening. He had a headache that had started on the bus on the way in, and it got steadily worse as his shift progressed. By eleven o'clock that night Storie was in no fit state to continue working and so called his supervisor, Mr Milton, at the Addiscombe Exchange. Permission to go home was given immediately and William Storie caught the number 115 bus, paying his one shilling fare to Thrale Road, Streatham. He had no memory of getting off the bus and could not say whether or not he went home that evening.

His next memory was of climbing through the window of the Tyrrells' house at Preston Road, Upper Norwood. He had with him a hammer, wrapped in a piece of paper. He thought it likely that he had taken the hammer to work to bang in a troublesome protruding nail, but he thought it was also possible he might have collected it from his home sometime between leaving work and reaching Preston Road. He could not say for sure what had actually happened. He remembered sitting in the kitchen of the Tyrrells' home, warming himself by the dying embers of the fire and smoking three cigarettes.

Jimmy Tyrrell woke in the early hours of 13 March, disturbed by a noise downstairs. He did not turn on the light but moved towards the bedroom door. This is what happened, in his words:

When I opened the door a hand shot out and hit me on the nose and made it bleed. Then I realized it was a tall man and he put his hands round my throat – I was standing up at the time. It was dark and I did not recognize who it was. I bit one of his hands and the next thing I knew I was on the ground. I then realized that the man was kneeling on my stomach and I rolled over and he put a knee on my back. I gradually worked myself under the bed and by this time I was screaming for help. As I worked myself out from under the other side of the bed the light went on and for a few seconds nothing happened and there was a lull. Then a heavy body jumped on the bed and I felt the springs pressing on my back and the person in the room was striking me with a hammer and hit me on different parts of the head, striking me six or seven blows. I was still screaming for help and suddenly he stopped. I tried to get out from under the bed but it took me ten minutes to work myself up on to the bed, I was so exhausted. When I got on to the bed there was no-one else in the room. While he was in the room the person who attacked me said, 'Stop shouting.' I recognized the voice.

Jimmy Tyrrell was too weak to leave his bedroom and lay helpless and bleeding until he was found a short time later by a police officer. It was then that he learned of the attack on his father. James Tyrrell had heard his son's cries for help and rushed into the bedroom to see what he could do. Storie turned the hammer on him. Despite seven deep lacerations to his scalp and a fractured skull, eighty-eight-year-old James Tyrrell managed to get away from his assailant, get away from the house even, and raise the alarm at the home of a neighbour, William Edwards.

When the violence was over, William Storie went back downstairs. Police described him as being in a kind of daze when they found him by the back door of the house. He openly admitted, 'I remember taking the rubber gloves off when I got downstairs so I must have been wearing them when I hit Jimmy and his father.' This striking candour typifies his behaviour following the attacks. Rubber gloves speak of premeditation, but he made no attempt to either hide or deny this significant detail. His preoccupation seems to have been not for himself but for his victims. 'Have you seen them yet?' he asked the police. 'Is Jimmy dead?' He was arrested and taken to Gipsy Hill Police Station. In his first interview he questioned Detective Inspector Harry Ireland about a motive for the attack, a strange inversion of normal procedure. 'Did Jimmy tell you why I did it?' he asked. 'Well, if he didn't tell you, I can't. Let me tell you what I can remember . . .'

William Storie was initially charged with causing grievous

Mayday Hospital c.1924. Croydon Local Studies Library

bodily harm to James Joseph Tyrrell, aged fifty-seven, and James Joseph Tyrrell senior, aged eighty-eight. This changed, however, on 29 March 1959. In the early hours of the morning James Tyrrell senior died at the Mayday Hospital of an acute pulmonary embolism, that is to say a blood clot blocking the circulation to the lungs. The origin of the clot was traced to the right calf and was, in the view of the pathologist carrying out the post-mortem, caused by his necessary confinement to bed. Since this confinement was a direct result of his head injuries, so must his death have been. The charge was now one of murder.

The central issue around which the entire prosecution case revolved was, of course, William Storie's mental state, both generally and at the time the attacks were carried out. Two different doctors were given access to him during his remand period, and they were able to compile extensive reports based on their interviews. They both found him to be intelligent and articulate, and they both felt that his lapses in memory were quite genuine. His discussions with them, as with his interviews with the police, were marked by frankness.

There was nothing in his family history to suggest mental illness. An average pupil at school in the West Country, he left at sixteen to try his hand at several jobs before joining the Post Office in 1938, and the Corps of Signals in 1939. He resumed his career at the Post Office immediately after the war. The only significant element of tension in his life was traced to his unhappy marriage. He married in 1935, and although he described his wife as 'a good woman, a good wife and mother', their relationship was overshadowed by her constant complaints and what he saw as her neurotic tendencies. He planned to leave her when their only daughter was independently settled, but in the meantime tried to bear the situation without retaliation. His own feelings of resentment were kept bottled up and in the years preceding the murder his headaches worsened.

At first the doctors suspected epilepsy but an examination by electro-encephalograph proved inconclusive. The other possibility was of hysterical dissociation, or fugue. This condition is marked by uncharacteristic behaviour, often accompanied by loss of memory and can sometimes follow a traumatic experience. One curious incident that supports this diagnosis occurred about eighteen months prior to the murder. As on the night of the attacks, the incident began with a severe headache. Again William Storie left work early to go home, but found himself instead wandering along Victoria Embankment at one o'clock in the morning. He had no explanation or memory of how he got there, and could give no account of his time since leaving work. He thought he had probably mentioned this puzzling lapse of memory to his wife, but he seems not to have been unduly worried by it. He certainly did not think it necessary to seek medical advice.

The conclusion of the examining doctors was that William Storie was fit to plead and to stand trial. There was, in the view of the Principal Medical Officer at Brixton Prison, no reason to believe that Storie did not know right from wrong at the time of the attacks, but his opinion was:

> *It is well within the realm of probability that he was in a mental state of partial hysterical dissociation and that this caused such abnormality of mind and was of such intensity as to be pathological and that it substantially impaired his mental responsibility for his acts.*

These findings were echoed in the other report, submitted by J B S Lewis MD. In it he stated that 'there is ample evidence for arguing diminished responsibility on psychiatric grounds.'

There was no disputing that the injuries inflicted on the father and son were severe. The more serious injuries were sustained by James Tyrrell senior, who needed between thirty and forty stitches to his head. Nor was there any question that these injuries had been inflicted by William Storie. The only real issue was the mental state of the accused and it seemed clear in the light of the evidence that a charge of manslaughter was more appropriate than that of murder. Although Storie did not take the stand during his trial, the judge, Mr Justice Barry, gave him the opportunity to make a statement. In a hesitant voice, William Storie addressed the court: 'The only thing I would like to say is to ask Mr Tyrrell junior if he could in time come to forgive me.'

William John Storie was found guilty of manslaughter and sentenced to four years in prison. The length of sentence reflected not so much a desire to punish, but the need to provide a suitable length of time for Storie to receive psychiatric treatment. The judge even hinted that he might be released before four years if the doctors felt he had recovered sufficiently.

Interviewed outside the Old Bailey after the trial, Jimmy Tyrrell spoke to reporters about William Storie. 'I do forgive him,' he said, 'and I bear him no malice.'

CHAPTER 6

Jealousy Without Cause:
Sarah Daws, 1896

She's been a-worrying on at me, but I loved every hair of her head.

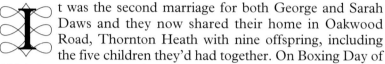

It was the second marriage for both George and Sarah Daws and they now shared their home in Oakwood Road, Thornton Heath with nine offspring, including the five children they'd had together. On Boxing Day of 1896 there was tension in the air, sparked off by George's near obsessive jealousy. In reality there was nothing to be jealous of: Sarah Daws loved her husband, and would not even go out without him. According to all those who knew her she was an utterly faithful and loving wife. But George spent his life in constant suspicion of infidelity.

Sixteen-year-old Elizabeth Daws remembered that in spite of the angry accusations made by her father, the evening ended in a more companionable atmosphere. Sarah read to George from the newspaper, and they even went out for a short while together to visit some acquaintances. When they returned George sent Elizabeth out for two quarts of 4d. ale and half a pint of Irish whiskey and by bedtime they were all the best of friends. So when Elizabeth retired at ten o'clock, she expected a peaceful night. Some time after midnight, however, she heard a thump, like the sound of something dropping to the floor, coming from her parents' bedroom next door to her own room. The eleven-week-old baby, who slept in Sarah and George's room, began to scream, alerting everyone to the fact that something was dreadfully wrong in the way that only babies can. Elizabeth got up, filled with a sense of unease. She tried to open her parents' bedroom door but it was locked; she knocked and called out to her stepmother, but it was her father who came out, carrying the baby. He thrust it into Elizabeth's arms, and asked her to keep it quiet in the other room. It was then that Elizabeth saw blood on the baby's night gown. She asked her father about it, but all he said was, 'Don't you tell stories.' She followed him downstairs, hardly able to make out what was happening.

'What's the matter with mother?' she asked.

'She has fainted, and I am going to get some milk.'

And with a warning to Elizabeth not to go into his bedroom, he left the house.

George, of course, had no intention of going for milk. It was urgent help he needed and so he walked the distance to his brother's house in Addiscombe as quickly as he could.

'Alf, come here; I want you a minute,' he called out to his brother, Alfred. It was 1.30 in the morning by now and he had disturbed everyone in the house in Cross Road. Alfred and his wife Emma answered the door.

'What have you done, George?' she asked.

'I've killed her.'

'Killed who?' asked Alfred.

'Sarah.'

'You have not; tell me the truth. What have you done?'

'I have dashed her brains out with a hammer and cut her throat.'

'For God's sake, tell me the truth; tell me what you have done?'

'Will this convince you?' said George, as he held out his blood-stained cuffs for his brother to see.

It was sufficient to convince Emma that the situation was serious and that she should see for herself what had happened. Without waiting for further explanations she went with one of her sons, who was a soldier, to the house in Oakwood Road. When Emma Daws and her son Albert reached number 14, they went straight to the marital bedroom where Sarah lay on her right side, still in her nightdress, covered in blood. Albert went to summon the police immediately, and returned a very short time later with PC Wilson.

Elizabeth had disobeyed her father's last instructions. She had gathered up the other children, who by this time had been disturbed from their sleep, settled them in the kitchen and gone into her parents' bedroom. She was standing over her step-mother's body when Emma arrived.

The sight was appalling. Sarah's throat had been cut and the top of her head was congealed with blood. The bed was also covered in blood, as were Sarah's nightclothes, and at the foot of the bed lay a blood-smeared coal hammer. The razor had been thrown into the fireplace.

The post-mortem later revealed that Sarah's throat must have been cut first, as there were slashes on her hands and arms where she had attempted to defend herself. Dr Robert Henderson, who carried out the post-mortem, reported that 'the throat was so cut as that the carotid and all the principal arteries of the neck were severed – I also found that the skull had been fractured.' The deeper of the two cuts to the throat had nicked the spine.

Back at Alfred's house, the two brothers were trying to come to terms with what had happened. George went to the washroom to remove the bloodstains from his clothing, but couldn't wash them out. He scrubbed at his cuffs and the knees of his trousers until Alfred stopped him.

'It's no use trying to wash it off, George – you can't get it out. Never mind – let it go.'

George's mind was rolling over and over the night's events. He could not remove the bloodstains from his cuffs any more than he could remove the image of Sarah from his mind's eye. Alfred took him out for a walk in Cherry Orchard Road, to try to clear his head, but understandably their conversation churned over the same thing. Alfred was still struggling to understand why it had happened.

'She has been a-worrying on at me, but I loved every hair of her head,' was all the explanation George could give at that point.

They had to decide what to do next. Back at the house in Cross Road, George decided he must face the consequences of his actions, and asked Alfred to go with him while he gave himself up. But it was unnecessary to go anywhere as the police were already on their way to him. George made his preparations. He gave

Alfred his bank book, showing a more than healthy balance of £210, as well as £60 worth of gold and silver. He asked Alfred to look after this for him in case he should need it 'to help him over his struggle'. He then gave Alfred his watch, telling him to 'keep that in memory of me'. The chain he handed over 'for little Herbert in remembrance of me'. Herbert was his eight-year-old son by Sarah.

Inspector Parks arrived at 2.45 and arrested George Daws for the wilful murder of his wife Sarah.

'I'll go quietly,' George answered. 'I know what it is for. Let me get my coat.'

Cross Road, where George Daws's brother lived. Croydon Local Studies Library

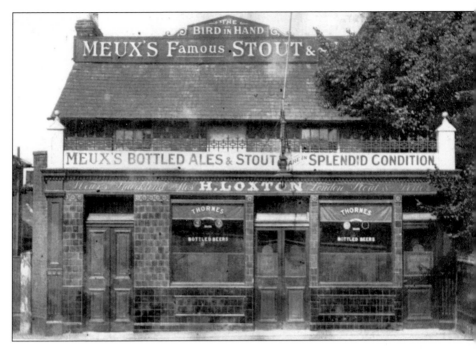

The Bird in Hand public house, run by George Ward. Croydon Local Studies Library

On the way to Croydon Police Station George spilled out his story 'all in one breath': 'This is all through Mr Ward, of *The Bird in Hand*. He's hounded me. He has paid them to keep me in tow while he has been intimate with my wife.'

For nearly two years George had nursed his obsessive jealousy. The previous year he had focused his fears on his own eighteen-year-old son by his first wife, convincing himself that George junior was making inappropriate advances towards Sarah. He had returned home one day to find them sitting together on the sofa, and had constructed an entire tale of infidelity around it. He said he knew Sarah had been going to the boy's bedroom and as a consequence threw him out of the house, in spite of protestations of innocence from both his son and Sarah. Thereafter he would periodically search the pockets of the other children, in case George junior was trying to slip secret notes to Sarah.

His attention then turned to George Ward, the keeper of *The Bird in Hand* beerhouse in Sydenham Road. Why his jealous mind singled out this particular gentleman, no one could say – Mr Ward did not even know Sarah. But George worked up a story in his own head that Sarah used rags hung at the windows to signal to

Mr Ward that George was out of the house. Elizabeth, however, testified that it was George himself who put the rags up in the window. She explained to the court:

> *On the Monday before Christmas Day he behaved very strangely . . . . He went upstairs and hung my little brother's tie outside the window of my mother's bedroom. He put a rag outside the back bedroom window, a blue bag in the wash-house window, and an old piece of blue silk in the window of the front sitting room. . . . My mother asked him what he put the rags in the windows for, and he said, 'They are signals.' He was quite sober when he said that.*

He also believed that other men kept watch on the house so that the couple could meet in privacy, and he began searching the cupboards for such men on his return from work each day.

In June 1896 George had been charged before the Croydon Borough Bench with assaulting his wife. In his now customary fit of jealous rage, made worse by alcohol, he had hit Sarah in the mouth with his fist, cutting her lip. He was ordered to pay two sureties of £10 each to keep the peace for six months, and was bound over for the same period. Sarah's death occurred within a few days of the expiration of this order.

In August George turned his violence on himself. He came home one evening, after having been drinking and told Sarah, 'Mother, this is the last night I shall be with you.' The following day he was very restless, pacing up and down the room, and in the afternoon he said simply, 'Goodbye, Sarah. I've done it.'

'What have you done?' she asked.

He told her to look under the toilet table in the bedroom and she found four empty penny bottles which had contained laudanum. She immediately went for the doctor, Dr Warren, leaving the children to watch over their father. The doctor administered an emetic and warned Sarah that George might attempt this again; she should watch him carefully. From that moment on, if Sarah found George with a razor she took it away from him for fear that he would harm himself. It is both sad and ironic that it was Sarah herself who ended as the victim of the razor.

Dr Warren gave evidence at George's trial that at the time of the attempted suicide he considered him to be insane. Several members of George's family testified that he was a loving and good husband, but that he behaved strangely at the change of the moon, a characteristic thought to mark the lunatic. Dr James Scott, the medical officer at Holloway Prison, confirmed to the court that in his opinion George suffered from insane delusions and was insane at the time the crime was committed, that he still had suicidal and homicidal tendencies and that he was in no fit condition to appreciate the nature of his actions. The jury found George Daws guilty of the crime of murdering his wife, but declared him insane. He was detained at Her Majesty's pleasure.

Sarah Daws's funeral was a simple affair. A large crowd of mourners came to Croydon Cemetery to offer their sympathy and all Sarah's children and stepchildren, now under the guardianship of their aunt, were present. But the most touching sight was the figure of Elizabeth Daws, standing over the grave of the woman she liked to call mother, carrying the youngest member of the family, barely three months old, in her arms.

CHAPTER 7

The Girl in the Candy-Striped Dress: Edwina Taylor, 1957

The law protects animals. It must also protect innocent children . . .

All parents have, at some point or other, momentarily lost sight of their child: in the park, at a crowded supermarket checkout, perhaps even at the school gates. For most the breathless moment of panic is short-lived and the little figure toddles back into view. But for the truly unfortunate few the panic goes on until the parents are faced with that ultimate horror, the loss of their child.

On the morning of Saturday, 31 August 1957, four-year-old Edwina Taylor and her brother were playing at a local recreation ground with friends Margaret and Yvonne Ward, ten and eleven years old respectively. At about 12.20 Edwina left with her three-year-old brother, Mark, to walk towards their home in Tudor Road, Upper Norwood, stopping as they went at the sweet shop in Belvedere Road. Today we might feel a sense of surprise at the thought of a three- and four-year-old being out unaccompanied, but history should be viewed within the context of its time, and this was nothing unusual for the 1950s.

They bought a threepenny ice cream each and walked back hand-in-hand to their home. Ten minutes later their father, Edwin, after whom Edwina was named, saw them in the front garden playing quite happily on their tricycles, but when at 12.50

Edwina's brother, Mark, with Yvonne and Margaret Ward.
Croydon Advertiser

their mother, Marguerite, called them for lunch, only Mark came running in. Marguerite and Edwin Taylor searched up and down the road, looking in any nooks and crannies where their daughter might be playing, but there was no trace of her. Their panic deepened as they realized this was not just mischievousness: Edwina was missing.

The police took the case very seriously from the onset. The first few hours of a search of this sort were known to be crucial and a full description of the girl was circulated to all local stations as well as to Scotland Yard. All building sites, derelict buildings and waste grounds were checked, and detectives knocked on the front door of every house in the area hoping for some piece of information, however small.

The next six days saw a full-scale hunt for Edwina, involving more than 100 police officers. In charge of the operation was Detective Chief Superintendent John Capstick, known to the underworld as 'Charlie Artful'. He was a quiet man, always recognizable from the pipe in his hand and the rose in his buttonhole, but he was also experienced in murder investigations. The control centre of operations was at Gipsy Hill Police Station, and there sat Edwin Taylor for lengthy hours, giving police any scrap of information that might help. They were working on two possible theories: firstly, that Edwina had been taken by a woman who desperately wanted a child of her own, or, more worryingly, that she had been abducted by a man who might have been driven by sexual motives.

Alsatians from the police dog training centre at Hendon were brought in to scour the area. The search covered the grounds at Crystal Palace, the old golf course at Norwood, Streatham Common, and then on to Sydenham, Penge and Forest Hill. No woodland area, derelict ground or building site was overlooked. Late on Monday evening, there was a development.

The case had naturally received a lot of media attention, and all the locals were by this time aware of the search for Edwina. So an incident that might otherwise have gone unreported came to the attention of the police. On Friday, 20 August, the day before Edwina went missing, a pretty, blonde, eight-year-old girl named Yvonne was approached by a man outside the sweet shop in Belvedere Road. He asked her if she would like a ride in his car and offered her some sweets. Very fortunately for Yvonne she refused and ran away. It was a narrow escape. But she was able to give the police a general description of the man who had tried to lure her away. He was dark-haired, of medium build and wore a dark suit, she said.

The following day the hunt intensified. Two hundred soldiers from the Royal Signals swelled the numbers of those searching for both Edwina and now also for the man they feared had snatched her. Following different leads the investigation stretched as far as Devon and even Amsterdam. Then on Thursday, 5 September, shortly after four o'clock in the afternoon, her body was found, just a few hundred yards from her house.

Two CID officers, DC Ronald Street and DC Jim Cruse, had been searching in empty houses around Upper Norwood and Penge. They checked a house in St Aubyn's Road, close to St Aubyn's church. The house was divided into flats but the basement had not been occupied for three to four years. And it was here, in a coal cellar, that they found Edwina. Chief Detective Inspector Capstick arrived at the house within minutes, closely followed by police photographers, fingerprint teams and two pathologists. For the remainder of the day detectives carried out

St Aubyn's Road. Croydon Local Studies Library

Edwina Taylor. Croydon Advertiser

interviews with the families living in the other flats in the house, as well as with the immediate neighbours. By the time Edwina's body was carried out draped in a faded green cloth, crowds had gathered outside the house.

Dr David Haler, one of the two pathologists summoned to St Aubyn's Road, later carried out the post-mortem at Mayday Hospital. He disclosed that her death had been caused by a fracture to the vault of her skull and strangulation. Although she was fully clothed when found, it was at first feared that Edwina had been sexually assaulted prior to her murder; thankfully, this proved not to be the case.

Within a matter of days of the discovery of Edwina's body, thirty-one-year-old factory worker Derrick Edwardson walked into Wealdstone Police Station and confessed to the murder. He lived with his wife in the flat above the basement in St Aubyn's Road and had been interviewed on the day the body was found. Fair-haired and of small frame, he did not fit the description given by Yvonne, the little girl approached outside the sweet shop. But Edwardson volunteered to write his own statement for the police, calmly answered all questions, and awaited his fate with resignation. His motive for the killing remained unknown.

Crowds of more than 400 people gathered outside Croydon Magistrates' Court to jeer at the self-confessed child murderer, and courtroom number one was filled beyond normal capacity, with people standing in the gangways to view the proceedings. Edwardson was ordered to appear at the Old Bailey and as he left the court the crowd erupted in anger. The *Croydon Advertiser* reported that 'as Edwardson left the dock, there were boos from some of the women in the public seats.' One vehicle leaving the courthouse was assumed to contain Edwardson, and the crowd blocked its path, banging on the side of the van and shouting abuse at the man they believed was inside. In fact the van was leaving to collect road signs, and police had to struggle to control the crowd to allow it to pass. Some time later Edwardson left for Brixton Prison to await his appearance at the Old Bailey in October. There

Neighbours line the street at Edwina's funeral. Croydon Advertiser

he pleaded guilty to the murder of four-year-old Edwina Marguerite Taylor, and was sentenced to life imprisonment.

After his conviction a series of previous offences came to the attention of the press. They included two charges of threatening to murder his wife, indecent exposure and a three-month prison sentence for indecently assaulting a five-year-old girl. The public was incensed. The debate on capital punishment for child murder hit the headlines and the Taylors were inundated with letters of support and condolence. The wave of opinion and an earnest desire to spare other families the misery that they had suffered prompted Edwin Taylor to head a campaign to change the law in the case of sex offences committed against children and to bring back the death penalty for child murder. He met with his Member of Parliament at the House of Commons to discuss the issue. He explained to the press:

> *I am past all bitterness, but I want the law changed. The law protects animals. It must also protect innocent children . . . I say immediately a man indecently assaults a child he should be segregated – removed from society and all contact with children.*

It is a debate that continues today.

If the public campaign gave a focus for the grief the Taylor family was enduring, they still had the pain of their loss to deal with in private. And the local community took every opportunity to demonstrate how far they shared in that grief. At Edwina's funeral women wept openly as they lined the streets near the Taylors' home. Police officers lined both Tudor Road and the one-and-a-half-mile route between St John's Church, Auckland

Road, and the Elmers End Cemetery where Edwina was finally buried. On top of Edwina's small white coffin lay a pillow of white chrysanthemums and lilies of the valley around a single red rose. The inscription read 'In loving memory from Mum and Daddy.'

CHAPTER 8

Poison After a Kiss:
Evelyn Norfolk, 1927

He told the elder of the two, a boy, to 'look after Mummy', while he went for help.

When Samuel Norfolk returned from work at half past eleven at night on Wednesday, 20 April 1927, he was surprised to find the front door of his cottage in Gibson's Hill, Upper Norwood, firmly locked. He knocked but no one answered. He rapped at the window; still no response. By now he was starting to feel anxious, and so he pushed back the catch with a knife that he always carried on him and climbed in through the window. He could not have been expecting the sight that met him. His wife, Evelyn, was sitting on the floor with her back propped up against an armchair; she appeared to be unconscious. A few feet away lay his brother, Ralph, just starting to regain consciousness. On the mantelpiece stood a bottle of Lysol, a corrosive poison, and two empty glasses.

There was foam around Evelyn's mouth, and brown stains on her chin, cheek and wrist. Ralph was making noises but all

Gibson's Hill. Croydon Local Studies Library

Gibson's Hill. Croydon Local Studies Library

Samuel's attention was focused on his wife. He lifted her into the chair, calling her name to bring her round and forcing salt water into her mouth in an effort to purge her of the poison. It did not make her vomit as he had hoped. Two of their three children came into the room, disturbed from their sleep by their father's cries of alarm and he told the elder of the two, a boy, to 'look after Mummy', while he went for help.

Samuel went for medical assistance to the home of Dr Smallwood, and was distraught to find him out. He next went to his parents' home in West Norwood and asked his father and sister to go to the cottage in Gibson's Hill, while he fetched the police. Things now began to happen more speedily. A sergeant returned with Samuel to the cottage and an ambulance was summoned immediately to take Evelyn and Ralph to Croydon General Hospital, although after an initial assessment they were transferred to Mayday Hospital.

Evelyn was in a worse condition than Ralph. Within a few days he was sufficiently recovered to be able to leave hospital, and was immediately arrested for attempted suicide, by law a criminal act until as late as 1961. It was different for Evelyn. Her body was in a state of shock and she had great difficulty in breathing. Her mouth was very sore where the lining had been burned away by the poison and she found it hard to swallow. By 22 April she was feverish with pains in her chest and doctors diagnosed bronchial pneumonia caused by the effects of the poison. Despite the best efforts of hospital staff to save her, Evelyn died on Monday, 25 April, five days after taking the poison. The inquest into Evelyn's death was now crucial, since under English law if two people entered a suicide pact and one survived, then the survivor was not only guilty of attempted suicide but of murdering the other person. At the very time when he must have needed the most support, Ralph Norfolk was facing the possibility of having to answer two very serious charges in a court of law.

The date set for the inquest into Evelyn's death, 30 April 1927, was hot and sunny. Ralph, as a person closely connected with the case, was obliged to attend the hearing. He sat in the courtroom silently crying as he waited for the Coroner to appear, but managed to compose himself as soon as the hearing started. He listened to his brother's evidence. Next the doctor was questioned about Evelyn's condition on arrival at the hospital, and about the findings of the post-mortem. Whether it was because of the heat or the nature of the medical questioning we do not know, but one of the jurors fainted and first aid assistance was necessary. The court was cleared for a moment and the Coroner asked for a window to be opened to allow fresh air inside. The hearing was being held in a first-floor committee room in the offices of the Croydon Union workhouse, and the windows overlooked a garden. The proceedings resumed.

Just as the Coroner was announcing the adjournment of the case, Ralph shocked the whole room by leaping from his seat and throwing himself head first through the open window. The drop to the ground was at least 30 feet. For a stunned moment no one moved. The press reported the next day:

> So quickly did Norfolk act that at first nobody in the court seemed to realise what had happened. All stood spellbound until the sound of the man's body striking the ground some thirty feet below was heard. Then with one accord, warders, policemen, pressmen and witnesses dashed from the room, down the staircase and round to the side of the building, where Norfolk was discovered lying huddled up with his head and shoulders in a currant bush, which had broken his fall.

Groaning with pain and only partially conscious, Ralph Norfolk was returned to Mayday Hospital for treatment, of his physical injuries at least.

It was several months before Ralph was able to face the charges laid against him. In July he answered the triple charges that on 20 April he murdered his sister-in-law, Evelyn Norfolk, and that he attempted to commit suicide at the same time, and again by

Croydon Union Workhouse, location of the offices where the inquest into Evelyn's death was held and where Ralph jumped out of the window. Croydon Local Studies Library

jumping through the window at the Coroner's Court on 30 April. He said simply, 'Yes', in reply to the accusations.

At Ralph's trial at the Assize Court in early July that year the jury listened to a statement Evelyn had made just before she died. In it she said:

> *On Wednesday, 20 April, I purchased a small bottle of Lysol. When I got home my brother's young lady, my brother and I and my brother-in-law, Ralph Norfolk, had a cup of tea together. After we had had the tea all the friends left except Ralph. I then took the cork from the bottle of Lysol and we had half each. I then kissed Ralph and we drank them together. This is all I can remember.*

But the mystery of this suicide pact was not how it was carried out but why. If Ralph and Evelyn had a romantic connection that went beyond the relationship of a brother- and sister-in-law, they did not admit to it. Ralph's version of events does suggest they were very close:

My sister-in-law suggested doing away with herself by taking Lysol.
I said, 'Don't do that.' She said, 'I will do it!' As I am very fond of
her, I said, 'If you do it I will take it with you.' . . . We said goodbye
to each other and then drank the contents of the cup.

He did not mention the kiss.

In Evelyn's statement she said that it was her husband who had made her want to die. 'I was fed up with my husband,' she said, 'he was always gambling.' It seems a flimsy reason for taking one's own life, unless there was an underlying depression or another source of anxiety that she did not want to mention. Ralph did say that he often heard them arguing.

As for Ralph, the prison doctor had an opportunity to question him and assess his state of mind while he was on remand. There was evidence of a depressed state of mind, the doctor concluded, although whether this was due to the fact that he was facing a murder charge, or for some other cause, he could not say. The official reason was presented to the court by the counsel for the defence. 'It was to some extent due to drinking,' he explained, although only a couple of empty beer bottles were found in the room. But, he went on to say, 'the whole thing was that he got into an exotic state of mind, and yielded to a sudden impulse when he took the Lysol.' It falls short of a satisfactory explanation.

By profession Ralph was a gunner at the Royal Artillery Barracks at Shoeburyness. At the trial an officer from the barracks gave evidence of Ralph's good character. He was 'sober, steady and intelligent', according to the officer, although he had been in trouble earlier in April for being absent without leave. He had served in India where he twice had malaria.

Following the statement made by Evelyn before she died, the judge was obliged to recommend that the murder charge be dropped. 'One must be sure', he explained to the court, 'that the operative cause of the suicide is through the instigation of the other person.' Evelyn had bought the Lysol herself, had said several times that she wished to die, and she had poured out the poison for each of them to take. There was no evidence that Ralph had encouraged her – on the contrary he claimed he had tried to dissuade her.

The judge picked up on the idea that alcohol had been a primary cause of the suicide, although there is no real evidence of this. It is true that several bottles of beer had been consumed, but the small gathering of friends on the afternoon of 20 April had been served only with cups of tea. Drunkenness was the easiest explanation for this mysterious story, but it remains unconvincing.

The woman came and said she was going to poison herself, and it was the obvious duty of the prisoner to have taken the bottle away and dashed it on the ground. The prisoner must have been drunk. It was a bad business. The prisoner must be put away where he could get no drink, and then could come out and try to be what he had been before; a man of good character.

Ralph Norfolk was sentenced to twelve months' hard labour.

CHAPTER 9

Playboy Boss: John Shippey, 1991

His death, however, was not so glamorous.

Detectives investigating the murder of a Croydon businessman are unravelling his tangled sex-life for clues to his killer. The charred body of John Shippey, 47, finance director with leading Croydon car dealers, Doves Jaguar, was found in the boot of his burnt out Ford Sierra Sapphire last Wednesday night. The romantic businessman with a playboy image had been stabbed to death.

So reported the *Croydon Advertiser* on Friday, 27 December 1991. And it is true that the life of John Shippey might easily have jumped off the pages of a best-selling thriller. He tried to live a so-called 'jet-set' lifestyle with offshore bank accounts, expensive cars including a Porsche 911, two villas in Spain, a speedboat in the Mediterranean, several properties in the Home Counties and a number of mistresses. His death, however, was not so glamorous.

John was kidnapped from his home in Kent and taken in his own company car to a lock-up garage in Croydon. Here his hands

were bound behind his back with plastic cable ties, and his feet were strapped up with brown tape. Several layers of the same tape were wrapped around his mouth and two cotton wool pads were fixed to his eyes. It was very cold in the garage. He was left there for hours to fear the worst.

At some point in the afternoon a man arrived. He opened the front door of the car, clearly not expecting to find a person tied up there, but on the other hand he did not seem unduly surprised.

John Shippey. Croydon Advertiser

Perhaps he knew to expect something, but had not been quite sure what. The man left, to return some time later with a heater. He opened the car door so that Shippey could feel the benefit of the warmth and sat on the floor of the garage, waiting. What went through John Shippey's mind at this point we can only imagine.

At about nine o'clock the following morning a second man arrived. This was the man in charge of the operation.

'What's going on?' asked the first man.

'It's nothing to do with you,' replied the second. 'You've got nothing to worry about.'

The second man now took over. He shouted repeatedly to John Shippey that he should have paid, he should have paid her, and as he shouted he ripped the tape from his captive's mouth so that he could answer. Now terrified, Shippey was ready to agree to anything. Yes, he stammered, he would pay. But this apparently was not good enough. The man in charge now grabbed a knife from the roof of the car and thrust it into John Shippey's chest several times.

The first man was horrified by what he saw, and shouted at the second, asking what was going to happen now. 'It's OK,' came the reply. 'He's going to die.'

John Shippey's body was found in the boot of his burnt out company car in Warwick Wold Road, Merstham. The date was 18 December 1991, three days after he was last seen alive. He had to be identified from his dental records, as nothing else about him was remotely recognizable. And it was a strange course of events that took him from a champagne and caviar

Burnt out car where John Shippey's body was found. Croydon Advertiser

Doves Jaguar. Croydon Advertiser

lifestyle one moment, to such an ignominious death the next.

John Shippey's position as finance director for the Doves
Jaguar dealership in Croydon had earned him £35,000 a year,
nowhere near enough to support the lifestyle he wanted. He was
separated from his wife, and probably paid for the maintenance of
his twelve-year-old daughter. In addition to this he had a
£250,000 home which he shared with his live-in girlfriend, Jo
Watson, in Ightham, Kent. Then there were the villas abroad, the
other women apart from his wife and girlfriend, the speedboat and
all the material trappings he believed marked his success. It was an
expensive life to lead.

John Shippey was apparently highly regarded both socially and
professionally. The prosecuting counsel in his murder trial said
that he was a 'trusted, popular and well-liked man', who led 'a
complex financial and personal life'. Even his mistresses accepted
his infidelities with an affectionate shrug. Sue Hipperson, a fleet
administrator with Doves, had had an affair with Shippey and
described him in glowing terms:

> *He was lovely to everybody, generous and wanted to help everyone.*
> *He loved life and wanted to do everything and enjoy it. John's type*
> *of person just wants to enjoy life at the time. He was always jovial*
> *and jolly. I knew he would have other women right from day one,*
> *but it was never a problem. John lived life from day to day.*

So how exactly did John Shippey pay for this life he lived from
day to day? The *Croydon Advertiser* reported the explanation
given by the prosecuting counsel at the Old Bailey:

Shippey was concerned with at least four other companies, which he used to defraud Doves by using his position to transfer cheques and selling cars, then putting the money into his other companies. That money was used to fund an extraordinary lifestyle.

The police estimated that up to £800,000 had been used in this way. And John Shippey was indeed generous with this money. He spent large sums on the women in his life, paying off their credit card bills, buying large items such as furniture, and paying for mundane things too, like food and household bills. For Sue Hipperson he paid a £10,000 deposit for a house in Caterham on the Hill.

And then in 1991 Doves started to become suspicious about the financial state of the company. They had no idea of the extent of John Shippey's financial sleight of hand, and at this point still thought of him as a trustworthy employee. So strong was their support of him that following his death they offered a £10,000 reward for any information leading to the arrest of his killer. But back in the autumn of 1991 Doves had decided that certain irregularities in the company accounts needed to be investigated. It was time for John Shippey to get his business affairs in order.

Sue Hipperson was aware that John was trying to raise cash quickly to fill the holes in the accounts. He now needed to sell the three houses he owned or part-owned. She told the court:

In November 1991 he wanted to sell all three properties, plus the ones in Spain. He told me he desperately needed money in his bank account. He appeared to be desperate.

Included in the three properties she mentioned was the house in Ightham that he shared with his girlfriend, Jo Watson. This was the trigger for the events that followed. Jo's son Karl had never liked John Shippey and the thought that his mother's home was to be sold to extricate Shippey from the financial web that he had spun for himself served only to fuel Karl's dislike. The

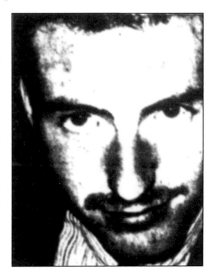

Karl Watson. Croydon Advertiser

kidnapping may have started out as a way of scaring John Shippey – Karl would not have wanted his mother to lose her home. Or perhaps Karl wanted Shippey to pay Jo her share from the proceeds of the sale – but whatever the original intention, it turned into something very sinister. It was Karl Watson who kidnapped John Shippey, and who with the aid of his friend, Bruce Cousins, held him captive in the lock-up garage in Croydon. It was Karl who yelled, 'You should have paid her!' and Karl who stabbed him repeatedly in the chest.

Detective Chief Inspector Beavis gave the court his theory of how Karl Watson's dislike of John Shippey turned into cold-blooded murder:

I am speculating but as young boys he and his brother were separated from their mother at the start of her relationship with John Shippey and that may have been the start of the animosity. And Shippey was known to carry large sums of money about and money was a very important factor in Karl's life. He was greedy .... Although there was nothing in his background to indicate that he was capable of murder, the more we got to know him the more we found out what he was really capable of. He was cold and calculating and with some degree of intelligence.

It took the police nearly two years to build a case against Karl Watson. He was a suspect from the moment that John Shippey's body was found, but there was insufficient evidence to bring a case to court. The investigation was made all the more difficult by the twists and turns of John Shippey's lifestyle. According to the police Shippey kept each strand of his life separated from the

Detective Chief Inspector John Beavis.
Croydon Advertiser

Croydon
Advertiser

Killer used gas to help burn corpse murder trial hears

others; each of his relationships and all of his business dealings were carefully structured, so that one person had no idea what John was discussing or doing with another. Detective Chief Inspector Beavis and his team worked relentlessly to untangle the various threads of this complex life. He said of Shippey:

> *I found him an enthralling man. He lived life in compartments and he didn't allow the people in each compartment to cross into others. As far as we can tell he lived like this for most of his adult life. To actually manage to live like that he had to be very intellectually bright. He had to know which particular part of his life he was living each day but he kept it up. But people accepted it. Some wondered about his wealth but John Shippey had the skill and the charisma to avoid awkward questions.*

The turning point in the investigation came in September 1992 when the role played by Bruce Cousins came to light. Cousins was arrested and he told the police everything: how Watson had kidnapped Shippey, stabbed him, and how the two of them had disposed of the corpse. At first they had not known what to do with the body. After bundling it into the boot of the car they drove it to a unit on the Milne Park Estate, New Addington. They later took it to Box Hill in Surrey with the idea of burying it in a field, but changed their minds. On their way back they passed

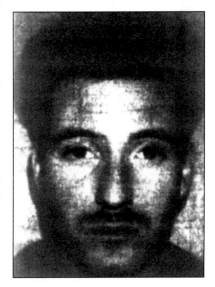

Karl Watson. Croydon Advertiser

Warwick Wold Road in Merstham, a quiet road that for some reason is a favoured site for the dumping and burning of stolen cars. It gave them the solution they were looking for. Three days after the murder, Karl Watson drove the car to Warwick Wold Road, packed gas cylinders around the body and set fire to it.

Even now the police were cautious. They needed physical evidence to link Watson to Shippey's abduction and murder, and eventually they found it. While searching the lock-up garages used by Watson, they found John Shippey's briefcase, still there after more than a year. In April 1993 Karl Watson was arrested for the murder of his mother's lover, and in December of the same year he was sentenced to life imprisonment at the Old Bailey.

CHAPTER 10

Madman or Murderer?
Thomas Cole, 1883

I believe him often to be violent without any cause.

T homas Cole had not yet reached his fourth birthday. He lived with his mother, father and brother, Richard, who was fourteen years old. The family was among the poorest in Thornton Heath. The father, James, was a brickmaker by trade, but had spent several short periods in prison for offences of drunkenness and violence; by August 1883 he had been unemployed for some time. His mother earned her living mending chairs, and Richard helped her in this. Their home reflected their poverty: the front door opened directly into the first of their four rooms, which were barely furnished. They slept on mattresses on the floor, and there were no chairs, only a shutter propped up on bricks for them to sit on. Buying food to feed the family was often difficult, but neighbours said the children never looked ill-nourished.

Richard left the house at about midday on Sunday, 19 August 1883, to run some errands. He returned at seven o'clock to find his parents in the midst of a furious argument, an argument that would result in the death of his three-year-old brother, Tom. His father was angry with his mother, and shouted at her, making wild accusations and threatening to 'kill the dear little innocent to leave something on her mind'.

After the shouting had subsided Richard said his parents went to bed quietly, only to wake an hour later at 9.30. Three-year-old Tom was asleep on the mattress with his mother and father. This time James Cole thought he could hear voices and screamed out in alarm. He asked his wife if she could hear the sounds and to appease him she said yes she could, but by this time she was distressed at his ranting and ran out of the house, too afraid to stay with him. James sent Richard to fetch his mother back. While they were both out of the house, James took Tom from his sleep and held him by the legs. From the gate in their small front garden Mrs Cole and Richard could see through the window into the first of their rooms. They saw James swinging Tom by the legs in a circle, banging his head against the wall as he whirled him about. Mrs Cole screamed in fear and ran into the house, shouting, 'Oh Jim, what are you doing? You've got my dear baby by the heels as if

Thornton Heath. Croydon Local Studies Library

you were going to dash its little brains out!' She grabbed the child from her husband and laid him gently down. She was distraught and hardly knew what to do. She ran to the door, sobbing and crying out that her husband had murdered her baby, but was halted in her tracks by a loud thumping noise. James had picked up Tom again, and was holding him upside-down, this time banging his head against the floor. He managed to do it once more before his wife could reach him, at which point he threw the toddler over his shoulder, dropping him in a heap on the floor. By this time Tom was unconscious and bleeding slightly on the right side of his head.

Screaming 'Murder!', Mrs Cole picked up her younger son and ran with him to her next-door neighbour, Mrs Harding. But other neighbours had been disturbed by the noise. Robert Gilbert heard the commotion and looked through the front door of the house to see James Cole swinging his son round by the legs, hitting the child's head against the wall as he did so. He saw Mrs Cole struggling with her husband to take the boy from him. He saw Richard Cole looking helplessly on from the front garden. Robert Gilbert pushed his way into the house, and while Mrs Cole was gathering up Tom in her arms, he dragged James outside. The men grappled for a while, Mr Gilbert hitting James, but the latter managing to break free and run away. James ran up the road barefoot, bare-headed and with no coat. He ran directly towards another neighbour, Thomas Knight, and announced that he 'had murdered his child'. Shocked, but with the presence of mind to take action, Mr Knight held on to James and said he was going to hand him over to a constable. This time there was no struggle.

Meanwhile, at Mrs Harding's house, the women were trying to revive Tom. He was unconscious and breathing lightly. The doctor was called immediately, and in the meantime Mrs Harding, her daughter and Mrs Cole tended the dying child. They washed him, put him to bed and waited for Dr Jackson. When the doctor arrived he noticed the bruising on Tom's face, head and arms, and slight bleeding from a cut by his eye. More ominous than the bruising, though, was the swelling on Tom's face and head. At a quarter past two in the morning, Tom vomited and had convulsions. By eight o'clock he was dead.

Richard was called on to give evidence at both the inquest and the Central Criminal Court trial. One small but crucial word in his evidence changed between the two. At the inquest he quoted his father as saying to his mother, 'I will kill the dear little innocent to leave something on your mind.' This was changed at the trial to, 'I will kill any dear little innocent to leave something on your mind.' The alteration of one single word matters because it indicates specific intent. If James Cole threatened to commit the very crime he went on to carry out, then it was a premeditated act of murder, and not an act of madness committed in the heat of the moment. And it was the proposition of the defence that James Cole was insane at the time of the murder. Did Richard understand the significance of this, and alter his testimony to save his father from the hangman's noose? Richard's evidence as to the nature of the argument between his parents also changed from the time of the Coroner's inquest to the Old Bailey trial. At the inquest he said that his father was angry with his mother because he had been given no food. He apparently threatened her life, calling her names. But his recollections at the trial were different. Then he laid great stress on the unusual behaviour of his father on the evening of the murder. He said he had accused his wife of plotting against him and of having illicit relations with other men. To the knowledge of Richard, and of friends and neighbours of the Cole family, these accusations were totally unfounded. James had supposedly yelled, 'I will give you something for putting people on to me, putting people in the cupboards and for putting men under the stairs and putting men in the cupboard to tease me, and trying to poison me.' Had Richard withheld that information at the inquest, or had he elaborated on it during the trial because he knew his father's life depended on it?

There is some reason to question James Cole's state of mind on that evening in August 1883, and indeed on several other occasions. Mrs Cole had certainly been worried about her husband's behaviour prior to the death of her son. On one occasion James became convinced that his wife was about to harm him while she was feeding Tom, and so he hit her on the head with a spoon, cracking her skull and leaving her permanently numb on one side of her face. She visited the family doctor, Dr Charles Smith, in May 1883 because she was afraid of her husband and wanted the doctor to visit him. In Dr Smith's words: 'I recollect the fact of my sending him to the workhouse infirmary because he was violent and his wife was frightened of him, but these symptoms were the result of drink, not insanity.' When questioned further, though, he did admit, 'I might have told his wife he was wrong in the head . . . [but] it was because he was violent that I sent him to the infirmary.'

The *Norwood News and Crystal Palace Chronicle* reported that on one occasion James Cole had been found wandering the streets of Croydon, and after appearing before the magistrates had been sent to the infirmary, 'but on the following day the symptoms of insanity passed off sufficiently to warrant his discharge.' The *Chronicle* went on to report:

On another occasion, after serving six months' imprisonment, he was seen walking about Croydon in an extraordinary condition, with the legs of his trousers torn into narrow strips and fastened at the knees. A resident of New Town, Upper Norwood, states that he once invited Cole to his house to sleep; that in the middle of the night his wife woke him in consequence of hearing strange noises in the lower part of the house; and that upon going down stairs to

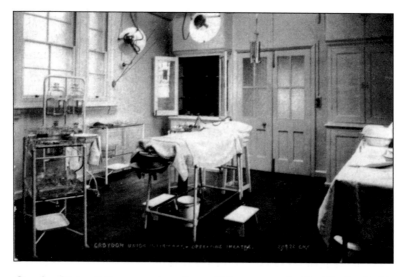

Croydon Union Infirmary, where James Cole was sent by Dr Charles Smith.
Croydon Local Studies Library

ascertain the cause of the noise, he found Cole busily engaged in trying to dig up the kitchen floor with a pickaxe.

Harriet Harding, the neighbour who helped Mrs Cole to nurse her son in his last hours, told a tale of violence rather than madness. She had often heard arguments next door, and on several occasions heard James Cole shout bad language and unpleasant names at his wife. 'I believe him often to be violent without any cause,' she told the court. She heard him say that 'sooner than a woman should do as she liked, he would sooner settle the lot.' This was said during the course of an earlier argument on the day of the murder, and it was an argument that left Mrs Cole crying openly in the back yard. Mrs Harding overheard it all – she recalled hearing Tom, who was upset at his mother's tears and tried to comfort her with the words, 'Don't cry, don't cry mama, I cry too.'

William Gilbert, the chaplain at Wandsworth Prison, visited James Cole on several occasions, both while the latter was on remand for the murder of his son, and previously when he had been in prison for offences of drunkenness and violence. In the opinion of the chaplain, James was 'of perfectly sound mind and understanding', at the times he saw him. Oliver Treadwell, the assistant surgeon at Clerkenwell Prison, shared the same view. He visited James frequently and formed the opinion that 'he appeared to be a sane man, as quiet and inoffensive a man as you would wish to have in the prison', with the exception of one occasion when his behaviour was so violent he had to be removed to a padded cell for two days. He had not 'presented any symptoms or delusions' during interviews, although he referred to his own delusional behaviour at home, when he heard noises and believed that people were hiding in the cupboards.

James's brother, Charles Cole, told the court of cases of suspected insanity in the family: of two uncles, one of whom 'drowned in a state of insanity' and of an elder brother who for years could not be left alone because he was not safe. He recalled an occasion twenty years previously when he had found James wandering in the streets in such a state of confusion that he had been unable to recognize members of his own family.

The final witness at the trial was Dr Thomas Jackson, both a medical practitioner and an Alderman of the Borough of Croydon. He had spent forty-five minutes interviewing Cole while he was in prison and came down firmly in support of the insanity plea. Cole told him that people had been trying to poison him, that his wife had been setting men to follow him, and that she had been pinching him in bed. He was also, at different times, convinced that people were trying to murder him or were writing unpleasant things about him in the newspapers. Dr Jackson had no doubts in his mind. 'I am quite certain that he is a typical lunatic, with dangerous delusions.' Then he warned, 'I say that no parish doctor ought to allow him to be abroad, because he is dangerous.'

It took the jury less than an hour to make up their mind on the case. They found James Cole guilty of murder, the sentence of death was passed, and without displaying any emotion, the prisoner left the dock. But the story did not end there. Cole's defence counsel, Mr Poland, and Alderman Dr Jackson, continued the fight for Cole's life. An appeal was lodged with the Home Secretary, and despite popular opinion that he should suffer the ultimate punishment for his crime, James Cole was granted a reprieve, and committed to Broadmoor prison hospital.

CHAPTER 11

Murder Without Motive: Johanna Hallahan, 1952

It was in quite a fit of laughter that I killed her.

The letter read out at the Croydon Magistrates' Court shocked everyone present. It was addressed to Mr Frank Hepworth, a senior Croydon probation officer, and had been written by twenty-one-year-old Frank Burgess, a porter at the Elgin Court Hotel, Addiscombe. He wrote:

If ever I have let anyone down it is you. I have committed a crime which I feel I should not have done, yet I could not prevent myself doing so. I don't know why I killed Joan but there it is. She took a long time to die but it was in quite a fit of laughter that I killed her. I have been back several times to look at her since she was dead. I have made the best of my last day.

The lack of remorse and sense of detachment evident in such a letter was hard to take in. The victim of this murder was twenty-three-year-old Johanna Hallahan, known to her friends as Joan. A strikingly beautiful girl, she had left her family in County Waterford, Ireland, to find work just two years earlier. She was working as a stillroom

ELGIN COURT HOTEL

PRIVATE AND RESIDENTIAL

SPACIOUS LOUNGES

BILLIARDS

MUSIC ROOM

H. & C.

GAS FIRES AND RINGS

NIGHT PORTER

★

ELGIN RAOD

EAST CROYDON

★

'PHONE : ADDISCOMBE 1000

★

CONVENIENTLY SITUATED WITHIN EASY REACH OF LONDON AND SURREY BEAUTY SPOTS

CLOSE TO 5 GOLF COURSES

Please apply to Resident Proprietor for Illustrated Brochure and Terms

Croydon Local Studies Library

maid at the Elgin Court Hotel when she was found dead in April 1952. According to the post-mortem she died of manual strangulation.

She and Burgess had been friends for the two months that they were employed together at the hotel. Joan was described by guests as a friendly girl, and even Burgess admitted that 'she was a nice girl and I liked her.' He also said that there was no romantic or sexual element to their relationship – they were friends and no more. In fact Joan had become engaged to a twenty-one-year-old Croydon man, Charles Hughes, the previous August and the couple planned to marry later in the year. Hughes, who lived in Cavendish Road, West Croydon, but worked as a kennelman at New Cross, was understandably devastated at the news of Joan's death, and struggled with the senselessness of her loss. They were supposed to be meeting on the day she died, and when she failed to turn up Charles was both perplexed and anxious. The following day he went to the Elgin Court Hotel in search of her, but it was her day off and the door to her room was locked and the blinds at the window pulled down. No one was able to give him any news of her.

On the day of the murder, 21 April 1952, Frank Burgess asked Joan to return some money that she had borrowed from him. He said she seemed annoyed that he wanted it back at such short notice, but she said she would try to return at least part of the sum owed. They met in her room after work for tea and cakes and she gave him back nearly 20 shillings. They sat talking for a while and he said that a few minutes later he realized she was dead on the bed. It was as simple as that – at least for Frank Burgess; Joan's broken fingernails indicate that she most probably fought back. He knew he had killed her, even recalled that he had done it while laughing, but could not explain his actions even to himself. 'I had no quarrel with her about money or anything else,' he later told police, 'but it was then that I must have lost my head. I know I must have done it, but I cannot remember how I did it.'

He sat smoking next to the body for some time, then drew the curtains, locked the door behind him and went to his own room to sleep. He returned several times the following day, just to check that she was dead. He then decided he did not want to look at the body any more and bundled her under the bed, covering her face with a blue overall. Before leaving for the last time he raided the gas meter in her room, then did the same to the meter in his own room. In the hotel reception was a collection box for the Croydon Darby and Joan Club, and he took this to his room so that he could steal the contents. Before leaving the hotel early on the morning of 23 April, he wrote his letter to Frank Hepworth,

The Elgin Hotel

NEAR EAST CROYDON STATION — At Elgin Road Roundabout

Daily Room and Breakfast
Weekly En Pension
Terms by arrangement

50 Bedrooms
Attractive Restaurant, Cocktail
Bars, Central Heating in Public
Lounges and Some Bedrooms

Private Rooms and Ballroom for
Weddings, Receptions, Conferences
Large Garden and Car Park

Telephones—
Reception Office:
01-654 1000 and 4646
Guests: 01-654 1581
Proprietors: Vokim Ltd.

Croydon Local Studies Library

the probation officer. In it he confessed that he intended to commit suicide:

> *I intend to take my own life as I could not face a trial. Maybe you think I am a coward or maybe not. Anyhow, I don't see it will make any difference as I hope to be asleep when you read this.*

Burgess may well have intended to kill himself (when arrested he had a bottle of aspirin in his pocket), but he said he later changed his mind. Instead he ordered a taxi at two o'clock in the morning of Wednesday, 23 April, and went to London to wander the streets.

At Piccadilly Circus he got chatting to a soldier, Private Raymond Baxter, and they went together to the Union Jack Club. Over a cup of tea Burgess took a piece of paper and wrote his name and address and Joan's name. He handed the paper to the soldier, and said, 'You just watch the newspapers for those names and you will know why I look so worried. It is serious. I could hang for it.'

The following day Burgess and Private Baxter went to London Zoo at Regent's Park, where they parted company when Baxter had to leave to catch a train. By this time, however, Joan's body had been found. When she failed to report for duty at 7.20 that morning and there was no reply at her door, the hotel proprietor, Mr J Peel, opened the window to her room. As soon as he saw the body beneath the bed the police were called.

Frank Burgess was arrested in London and brought back to Croydon Police Station for questioning. He offered no resistance and admitted to everything. He asked only that he be allowed to rest for a while then volunteered to tell the officers what had happened.

In the course of his trial, details emerged of a very troubled background. Frank Burgess had been born while his mother was a patient in a mental institution, and spent most of his childhood in an orphanage. While serving in the army in the Middle East he suffered a severe attack of typhoid before being discharged, principally on account of his mental instability. In February of the year in which he murdered Joan Hallahan, he was found in Redhill, Surrey, sobbing uncontrollably after having attacked a taxi driver for no apparent reason. To no one's surprise, defence counsel entered a plea of insanity.

The two doctors called by the defence supported this plea, but Dr Mathieson, the principal medical officer at Brixton Prison, said that although he agreed that Burgess showed evidence of a

Croydon Magistrates' Court. Croydon Local Studies Library

psychopathic personality, he believed him capable of understanding the criminal nature of his actions and that he knew it to
be wrong. Mr F H Cassels, defending counsel, used the fact that
there was no motive as evidence of insanity. 'Unless he was
abnormal,' he argued, 'what reason did he have for this attack? It
is a murder without motive.' In his summing up, however, the
judge, Mr Justice Streatfield, took a different view. 'The fact that
the prosecution do not know of a motive does not prove that there
was not a motive,' he told the jury. Within thirty minutes of
retiring the jury returned a verdict of guilty, but with a strong
recommendation for mercy on account of Burgess's mental state.
It was a recommendation that found no favour with the Home
Secretary, and Frank Burgess was hanged for the murder of
Johanna Hallahan in July 1952 at Wandsworth Prison.

CHAPTER 12

Seduced by the Devil: William Scawen, 1775

His mouth was drawn up as if he had a halfpenny in it.

O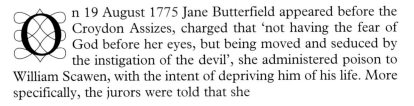n 19 August 1775 Jane Butterfield appeared before the Croydon Assizes, charged that 'not having the fear of God before her eyes, but being moved and seduced by the instigation of the devil', she administered poison to William Scawen, with the intent of depriving him of his life. More specifically, the jurors were told that she

> *at the said parish of Beddington, in the county aforesaid, did knowingly, wilfully, and feloniously, and of her malice afore-thought, mix and mingle certain deadly poison, to wit, solution of corrosive mercury sublimate in and with certain medicines and liquors, which had been at diverse times during the time above specified, prepared for the use of the said William Scawen, to be swallowed and drunk by him.*

Jane's history was an interesting one. As a young girl in her early teens she had been persuaded by an older woman to leave her family and to live with William Scawen, a wealthy man many years her senior. In the words of one of her friends:

> *At the age of fourteen, before she was capable of forming a proper judgement between virtue and vice, she was seduced from her parents by one of her own sex; brought to Mr Scawen; and, by a variety of artifices, prevailed on to continue in his house. Mr Scawen spared no expence [sic] in perfecting her education; and shewed her so many instances of friendship and kindness, that she sincerely loved him, and gave him many unquestionable proofs of her gratitude, fidelity and affection.*

In essence Jane had been seduced by William Scawen, and because of this her father disowned her. She was friendless and helpless and had no alternative but to take the offer made to her by Scawen, and live under his protection. In her words:

> *What could I do? To rely upon the promises of my undoer afforded some shelter; to retract from him, and throw myself naked and*

defenceless on the world, was a step, in my judgement at that time,
pregnant with greater mischief, if not my utter ruin.

The understanding between William Scawen and Jane
Butterfield was plainly stated. She would live with him at his home
at Woodcote Lodge, look after him and run his household, and in
return he would leave her the bulk of his estate upon his death.
She would therefore have had much to gain by his demise, but
appears to have become sincerely attached to him over time. Why
they did not marry is unclear – possibly for no other reason than
that Jane was William's social inferior. But it is evident that they
lived in mutual respect and affection for fourteen or fifteen years,
and that he made several wills principally in her favour.

Jane was good-natured – of 'uncommon openness of heart and
mildness of disposition', according to the friend who publicly
spoke up for her. And it was because of her sweet temperament
that she won respect and acceptance within the community of
Woodcote, despite her status as mistress rather than wife. She was
renowned for her charity to the local poor, and one example of her
compassion to others is demonstrated in her behaviour towards
another lady with whom William Scawen had once had an
amorous relationship. The lady in question, known only as Mrs F,
had a daughter by Scawen. He gave her a meagre allowance on
which to bring up the child, and her life was blighted by poverty.
When Jane heard of Mrs F's difficulties, she gave her an additional
£20 a year out of her own allowance, and when Scawen redrafted
his will in 1774 she persuaded him to leave his natural daughter
£7,000 rather than the £4,000 he had intended. These were huge
sums of money for the time, and Jane's behaviour over the will
was not that of an acquisitive person.

William Scawen had been ill for more than six years prior to his
death, and during this time Jane nursed him with care and
consideration. He suffered from severe rheumatism, among other
things, and in April 1775 took a tincture prepared by his apothecary, Mr Robert Cochran, to alleviate this, but stopped when it
caused an adverse reaction. He believed that the tincture
contained mercury. In May of that year he visited his doctor, Mr
Edmund Sanxay, for treatment of his rheumatism and for an ulcer
on his left arm. The doctor prescribed plasters and powders to be
put on the ulcerated arm, and a milk diet and a concoction of
sarsaparilla for the rheumatism. But William found himself unable
to continue with this last treatment as he complained that all his
drinks, including the sarsaparilla draught, had a distinctly metallic
taste. The illness that had begun when William took the tincture
persisted, and when the apothecary visited him at home in the

June, he began to grow suspicious. He did not believe that mercury taken in April could still be affecting his patient in June; someone, he felt, must have been administering further doses.

Mr Cochran, the apothecary, communicated his fears to William Scawen's sister, Lady Mead. He advised her to alert the doctor to the danger he suspected William to be in. Mr Sanxay attended William at his home on 16 June when the patient was too ill to go out. He had been intermittently feverish, nauseous, and his mouth was ulcerated. He also complained of excessive salivation. The doctor supported the apothecary's view that this could not possibly be the effect of medicine taken months previously, but he kept his suspicions to himself and tried several other remedies, such as bark draughts and chalk mixed into the patient's drinks.

Jane Butterfield was present during all the doctor's discussions with William Scawen, and it was left to her to implement the doctor's instructions. The brassy, metallic taste of which William complained in his drinks continued, and seemed to exacerbate the sickness. As Mr Sanxay later explained, 'He complained that always after he drank, his mouth was drawn up as if he had a half-penny in it,' but that it caused 'distress' rather than a distinct pain in his stomach. The doctor watched the situation closely. He checked that all liquids were boiled in silver rather than copper

Artist's impression of Jane Butterfield administering poison to William Scawen.
Croydon Local Studies Library

pots, and he advised Mr Scawen to swill any liquid round his mouth first to see if it had the brassy taste, before swallowing it. He also recommended that a nurse be hired, which Jane took exception to, viewing it as a slight on her own nursing skills. She argued that a nurse would be pointless, since Scawen would only accept help from her. But Mr Sanxay was adamant, and a nurse was hired.

Despite the fact that the doctor kept his suspicions to himself, rumour started to spread, and Lady Mead openly spoke of her brother's being poisoned by mercury sublimate. The nurse was now installed in the house at Woodcote, but she was never present when the doctor visited. Mr Sanxay's anxieties grew. He asked a colleague, Robert Young, a doctor experienced in treating patients with venereal disease, and therefore familiar with the side effects of mercury, to examine William Scawen. Mr Young felt the extreme soreness and ulceration on the inside of William's mouth was most probably due to mercury, and it was all the confirmation Mr Sanxay needed. He advised the patient to leave the house immediately and offered to take him to his own home. Naturally alarmed and concerned for his own safety, William accepted the doctor's offer and left his home immediately.

Although William was now safely installed at the doctor's house and beyond the reach of Jane's alleged poisoning, the ulceration in the mouth continued, and more significantly, so did the brassy taste in his mouth. Whatever his ailment might have been, he was now too far gone, and on 21 June 1775, under the care of Mr Sanxay, he died. At the

THE

LIFE

A N D

TRIAL

O F

JANE BUTTERFIELD,

For the WILFUL MURDER of

William Scawen, Efq;

AT THE

Affizes held at CROYDON for the County of SURRY

On SATURDAY the 19th of AUGUST 1775,

BEFORE THE RIGHT HONOURABLE

Sir SIDNEY STAFFORD SMYTHE, Knt.

Lord Chief Baron of h's Majefty's Court of Exchequer.

LONDON:
Printed by O. Truman, in the Strand.

Title page of The Life and Trial of Jane Butterfield. Croydon Local Studies Library

doctor's instigation, Jane was arrested for his murder.

The medical evidence given at the trial makes strange reading for the modern eye. They discussed at length the temperaments of the body and the salivation caused by mercury, as well as the ulceration of the mouth. Robert Cochrane, the apothecary, Edmund Sanxay and Robert Young gave their opinion in no uncertain terms, as might have been expected. However, another witness, Dr Saunders, was called to the stand and he, crucially for Jane Butterfield, testified that the symptoms might be attributable to other causes.

Court:	*Mention what other distempers will produce a salivation?*
Dr Saunders:	*In the first place, I would observe, that a salivation may arise from various causes, one of which is a paralytic state, a palsy in those parts which will produce frequently involuntary discharge of saliva, or a salivation.*
Court:	*Old people have frequently a relaxation of the throat, that they cannot swallow their spittle?*
Dr Saunders:	*They call them drivellers.*
Court:	*I apprehend that is from the weakness of the throat?*
Dr Saunders:	*Sometimes they can swallow, even when a salivation arises from a paralytic state of the parts.*

Dr Saunders then went on to give the case history of a woman who he supposed must have taken a mercury sublimate but whose symptoms arose from another cause entirely. And his testimony ended with his belief that such symptoms as William Scawen presented might well appear without the presence of mercury. Following this, three surgeons were called in defence of Jane Butterfield. They were all experienced in administering mercury, aware of its effects, and they all stated that the symptoms of salivation and ulceration could and did return without further doses of mercury being administered. In fact the third surgeon to be questioned said that William Scawen 'told me that from repeated venereal injuries he had taken mercury'.

In summary, then, William Scawen had possibly taken mercury in the tincture given by the apothecary for rheumatism. He may even have taken mercury for venereal disease. But it is evident that he had taken a series of concoctions for different ailments, and that no one truly understood the nature of his illness. The modern view of mercury poisoning is that ingestion of mercury salts, the corrosive sublimate referred to by the doctors in this case, can

Title page of the letter published by an unknown friend of Jane Butterfield. Croydon Local Studies Library

A

L E T T E R

T O

Mr. S A N X A Y,

Surgeon, in Effex-Street.

OCCASIONED BY

HIS VERY SINGULAR CONDUCT,

In the PROSECUTION of

Mifs B U T T E R F I E L D,

W H O

Was tried at the Affizes at Croydon, Aug. 19, 1775,

For P O I S O N I N G the late

W I L L I A M S C A W E N, Efq.

O F

Woodcot-Lodge, in the County of Surry,

A N D

HONOURABLY ACQU₄TTED.

―――

―――― Duris genuit te cautibus horrens
Caucafus, Hyrcanæque admôrunt ubera tigres.
VIRG. Æn. iv. 366.

L O N D O N,
Printed for G. KEARSLY, in Fleet-ftreet.
MDCCLXXV.

produce severe stomach cramps, vomiting and bloody diarrhoea. The inhalation or absorption of mercury through the skin produces the salivation of which William Scawen complained. Death usually results when the absorption of the mercury becomes concentrated in the kidneys: they stop working and the resulting build-up of toxins in the blood is lethal. Depression and personality changes generally occur prior to death.

Jane Butterfield did not speak in person in her own defence, but asked that a letter be read out in court. In it she described how she had been seduced at a time of innocence, but that she had come to love and respect the man who became her protector and, indeed, her family. Despite her initial fall from grace, her respectability shines through in the letter, as does her sincere regard for William Scawen. She writes:

> *I will thus publicly do him justice, that, except in the instances of our first acquaintance and conclusion of it, he sought all means to make me happy: nor was the improvement of my mind neglected; in this he faithfully supplied a parent's duty: to which I will add, that he was by nature generous, and, to myself, that generosity was unbounded. Judge then, my lord, what I must have felt when charged with a crime of the most shocking heinous nature! Not only of murder, but of murdering this benefactor and my only friend.*

Jane Butterfield escaped the gallows. As a result of her good reputation and the statement she made to the court, and in view of the widely differing medical opinions, she was found not guilty by the jury. However, Mr Sanxay was so utterly convinced of her guilt that while William Scawen was under his roof at the end of his life, he persuaded his patient to change his will, cutting Jane Butterfield out completely. Jane left the court a free woman, but now faced punishment of a different sort: extreme poverty and hardship for the remainder of her life.

CHAPTER 13

Intolerable Cruelty:
Una Pierce, 1963

We had our rows but she never got any serious hurt from me.

Dr Robert Moffat held his surgery in Brighton Road, South Croydon. On Tuesday, 17 September 1963 he saw a patient who gave him particular cause for concern. She was thirty-four-year-old Una Pierce and she was suffering from a number of minor but unpleasant injuries such as bruises to her upper lip, left thigh and right calf. More worrying, though, was her state of mind: she was distressed and highly anxious. Her husband had caused these injuries, she explained, and his violence was making her life intolerable.

We can piece together what happened on the night before Una's visit to Dr Moffat from various statements given to the police. Robert Shoulder, who lived next door to Una and Idris Pierce (known to his family as Ivor), said that on that evening in September he heard screams coming from the next-door garden at 33 Purley Road. He heard Una's voice saying 'No Ivor, no Ivor!', and Mr Pierce quietly telling her to come inside. He continued:

I next heard a terrific thump, sounding like a boxer punching a punch bag. Mrs Pierce then said, 'I'll come in Ivor.' I heard somebody being dragged along the passageway between the two houses, the back door of 33 was shut and then all was quiet.

The story from the other side of the fence sounded no better. In fact Idris Pierce's version of the same story has a chilling quality to it:

On Monday, 16 September she and I had a quarrel. I should say that she gave me a look which I didn't like, and I gave her a push. This was in our living room and she fell against a wall. She did not complain. She must have gone to our neighbours to complain because I saw her at their back door. I jumped over the fence and pulled her. She pretended to faint and I lifted her up and she grabbed the fence. She then fell on the fence and hurt her legs. We made up our quarrel but bad feeling started again between us on Monday, 23 September, when, upon my return from work she did not give me the usual kiss.

The reasons for the violence read as pathetically trivial, but underlying them was a strong emotion that Idris Pierce found hard to control: jealousy. Una had a part-time job at the Little Topper Café in Mead Place, Croydon, and she had recently become friendly with one of the customers. He was Godfrey Arthur Hone, known as Arthur to his friends, and he lived with his wife and two children in Sanderstead. There was no sexual relationship whatsoever between them, they both said, nor did he ever support her financially, but he had started doing little favours for Una, such as driving her to her sister's house, and on one occasion Idris suspected that the two of them had gone to the cinema together and then to a pub for a drink. Even Idris acknowledged that this was nothing more than suspicion but he found the situation hard to bear. Arthur Hone was an electrical engineer earning far more than the £14 10s. per week that Idris earned as a telephone engineer with the GPO in Purley. And Idris feared that Arthur's comparative wealth would impress Una so much that she would leave him. He did not understand that it was his own violent reaction to this fear that was driving Una away.

But the pattern of violence had been established in the Pierce household and it seemed impossible to break. And so the inevitable happened. Una left her husband on 30 September

Purley Road, 1959. Croydon Local Studies Library

1963, and moved into lodgings on her own in Harold Road, Upper Norwood. She decided that it would be less unsettling for their two daughters, Ann aged eight and four-year-old Linda, if they remained in the family home; she saw them whenever she could.

The case preyed on Dr Moffat's mind. He contacted Mr Pierce and asked him to visit the Brighton Road surgery on 4 October. The doctor confronted him with the issue of domestic violence. 'I was very cross with him,' the doctor later explained, 'and I gave him a piece of my mind for having caused these injuries to his wife.' He went on:

> *I thought he was suffering from a reaction of a nervous kind. He had obviously lost weight and I thought at the time he was genuinely sorry for all he had done. He promised me that if I could persuade his wife to return to him he would never strike her again. . . . I told Pierce that this was the third episode to my knowledge and that, despite all his reassurances, if it recurred I would certainly have to report the matter.*

The doctor, believing Idris's remorse to be sincere, arranged appointments for 8 October to discuss the situation with Una and Idris, at first separately and then together. His aim was to try to bring about a reconciliation. Idris promised to do anything to get his wife back, but Una decided that having broken away from the violence, she could not consider returning to it. The doctor felt he had done all he could.

In Idris's mind, however, his behaviour was not so bad. 'During all this time my relations with my wife were quite normal,' he later told the police. 'We had our rows, but she never got any serious hurt from me; I think about two black eyes on different occasions.' It is likely that this is an underestimate of the injuries inflicted on Una Pierce, but even if it were an accurate statement, such blasé acceptance of violence towards a spouse jars on the twenty-first-century ear.

At half past three on Saturday, 2 November 1963 Arthur Hone met Una and her daughter Ann at West Croydon Station and drove them to within about 500 yards of the family home in Purley Road. He arranged to meet Una again at five o'clock at the *Swan and Sugarloaf* public house. He never saw her again.

Idris had sent Ann to her mother that day to try to persuade her to come home to the family. Una was not prepared to do this but she did want to see her daughters, and so returned with Ann to Purley Road. Idris took his opportunity – he wanted to persuade her to stay but as so often happened he turned to violence rather

West Croydon station. c.1958. Croydon Local Studies Library

Swan and Sugarloaf *public house.* Croydon Local Studies Library

than words to further his cause. He told their younger daughter Linda to go upstairs to change her clothes; Ann was already in her bedroom. He then took a large carving knife out of the sideboard, initially just to frighten Una, he later said, but the thought came to him that if he couldn't have her, then neither would anyone else. He struck out with the knife eight times, into her chest, shoulder and the side of her head. Some of the blows were delivered with such force that they penetrated the bone of her ribs and her skull. One thrust pierced her heart. It seemed to Idris that she stood still for endless seconds. Then she fell, tumbling backwards over a chair so that she landed with her head on the floor and her legs tipped up on the chair. The girls heard the noise and came downstairs. 'What have you done to her?' Ann asked her father. They were both in a state of shock and Idris had the presence of mind to tell them to go immediately to 'Auntie' Pat's, Mrs Lowrie, who lived at 37 Purley Road. They did as they were told, and then Idris rushed to the nearest telephone box and dialled 999 for an ambulance. But it was too late to do anything to save Una's life.

At the police station Idris poured out his story. His words came thick and fast, as if he needed to empty himself of the burden of what he had done. He spoke in the same rattling way to the medical officers who examined him while on remand. Dr F H Brisby noted after an interview with Idris Pierce:

> *He was not only willing to discuss the case but simply poured out a narrative. It is almost an understatement to say he was garrulous. It seemed at times as though he were trying to make the case against himself as black as he possibly could.*

At the Old Bailey trial in December 1963, Idris Pierce's plea of not guilty of murder on the grounds of diminished responsibility was accepted by the court. But he was found guilty of

STAB WOUNDS 'OF GREAT VIOLENCE,' COURT TOLD
Man accused of murdering wife

Croydon Advertiser

manslaughter. The judge, in passing sentence, reminded him that while it had been established that he was suffering from some abnormality of mind at the time the crime was committed, he was by no means absolved of responsibility for his actions and that a custodial sentence of seven years reflected the seriousness of the crime. The girls, Ann and Linda, were now without both their mother and their father. But they were not without family altogether and they went to Dolgellau in North Wales, where Una's brother, John, faced the difficulties of caring for two children whose lives had been devastated by domestic violence in its most extreme form.

CHAPTER 14

Clyde Road Shooting:
Anthony John Everitt, 1957

He keeps on at me and won't let a man live.

It is rare for a school report to capture so concisely and accurately the essence of a pupil's difficulties in life, but the report written by the head teacher of Davidson Road School about Morris Edward Ware showed remarkable insight. Although Ware was 'honest, generally co-operative and polite', wrote Mr J T Jones, he was also 'of hasty temper . . . unstable, unpredictable in his behaviour, incapable of comprehending when he was in the wrong and often showed signs of hysteria'. Then, significantly, he added, 'He formed deep friendships but with others maintained open hostility.' These were characteristics that Morris Ware carried with him into adulthood.

His teenage years were troubled. A below-average pupil with a pronounced stammer, he left school aged fifteen and for the next few years wandered in and out of a series of labouring jobs. He was never sacked, indeed was often described as a good worker,

Davidson Road School, c.1960. Croydon Local Studies Library

but he quickly became bored and left, often within a few weeks of starting a job. And there were difficulties at home. He was a Teddy Boy and his parents disapproved of many of his friends, regarding them as 'bad company'. On two occasions his father threw him out of the family home, once after Ware threatened certain members of the family. At eighteen he refused to register for National Service until his father became insistent – only then did he agree to register for coal mining work. In May 1955 he was called up and was posted to the Royal Corp of Signals as a driver, but even this did not last. He was invalided from the army in November of the same year, diagnosed with 'post-traumatic epilepsy'. This diagnosis was later questioned.

So Morris Ware reached the age of twenty with next to nothing that was stable in his life, least of all himself.

On 4 January 1957 he shot, at point-blank range, twenty-one-year-old Anthony John Everitt, and ran off, leaving him to die on the pavement in Clyde Road, Croydon. Ware was arrested by police the next morning. In the police car he broke down in tears and told the arresting officers, 'I did not mean to do it – he has been crowding me. There was a flash and I ran off . . . I am sorry for his wife and baby.' He explained that he had a gun on him because he was trying to sell it. But, he said, he had never intended to deliberately seek out Everitt or to use the weapon on him. At the police station he explained further.

Everitt had, according to Ware, been taunting him for some weeks. He was apparently casting about rumours that he, Ware, had committed certain thefts, when in fact they had been committed by Everitt. He openly jeered at him in the streets, calling him names like 'big shot' and 'chicken', and had even visited Ware's girlfriend at her home to spread more lies and rumours. 'He keeps on at me and won't let a man live.'

On the evening of the murder, Morris Ware had been to the cinema with his girlfriend, Ann Griggs. His landlady testified that they returned to his room between seven and eight o'clock, and that they then spent over an hour in her living room listening to the gramophone.

Morris Edward Ware. Croydon Times courtesy of the Croydon Advertiser

Anthony Everitt and his wife Valerie.
Croydon Times courtesy of the Croydon
Advertiser

He left the house for twenty
minutes or so to go to a nearby
café, but returned in time to
walk Ann home. They left
together shortly before ten
o'clock, and as they went out
the front door he called affectionately to his landlady, Clara
Quantrill, 'I won't be late,
Mum.' He liked to call her
'Mum'.

He parted from Ann at a quarter past ten in Gladstone Road,
and from that point on we have only Ware's word for what
happened:

> *I was walking along Lower Addiscombe Road and I walked into
> Clyde Road. . . . I didn't know he was just behind me. I turned
> when I got half way up there and he started laughing and said, 'Are
> you looking for me?' and I told him what he had been saying to me
> girl and I was talking to him and he grabbed hold of me round the
> neck and I jumped back and me shirt tore. I stood back and said,
> 'Stand where you are.' I was bluffing him. He said, 'You're nothing
> chicken.' I started to sweat and shake, me head was going round. I
> had the gun in me pocket. I don't know what happened, suddenly
> there was a blinding flash and all I can remember is running up the
> alleyway to the church. . . . I didn't try to run nor nothing. I was
> going to give myself up.*

In fact what he did was to throw the gun into the churchyard of
Addiscombe Parish Church and walk away. A little before seven
o'clock the following morning, Saturday, 5 January, he appeared
at the home of a friend, Louisa Shepherd, looking dishevelled and
dirty. She gave him a clothes brush and a cup of tea and his explanation of his state was that he'd beaten up Everitt with a bottle and
couldn't stop because the police would probably be after him.
They were indeed, but for murder, not assault.

The reality of Morris Ware's relationship with Tony Everitt
was rather more complex than he first admitted to the police on
his arrest. They had tried to set up in business together dealing in

Clyde Road, 1957, where Everitt was shot. Croydon Advertiser

old cars and scrap metal. But Everitt had allegedly attempted to cheat Ware out of his share of the profits on the sale of an old car. According to a friend, this had put them on 'fighting terms'. Then the two of them were arrested together on 10 November 1956, on a charge of receiving a road fund licence knowing it to have been stolen. They were remanded on bail and were due to appear at Wallington Magistrates' Court on 9 January 1957. The murder took place just five days before the scheduled court appearance.

It seems that Anthony Everitt had been trying to get Morris Ware to take sole responsibility for the offence, and had been working with his solicitor to this end. Ware was both angry and distressed about this. On 12 December, about four weeks before the murder, Ware telephoned DC William Fraser at Mitcham Police Station and asked for a meeting somewhere in Croydon, so that they could discuss the case. In fact they met at Mitcham in the presence of another detective, and Ware offered to give the police information about certain thefts and burglaries that had taken place, presumably in return for lenient treatment over the road fund licence case.

At the Old Bailey murder trial the motive for this meeting was more fully explained. A friend of Ware's, Edward Quantrill, gave the following evidence. He refers to Morris Ware as 'Mole':

Mole thought Tony had been grassing on him because four bogeys came down from Norwood to see him. Tony was wild about Mole

Addiscombe Parish Church in 1959 where Morris Ware disposed of the murder weapon. Croydon Local Studies Library

talking about him and there was a lot of bad feeling between them. Mole said if he can't do it with his fists he'll do it down the Law Station. Mole meant that if he couldn't beat Tony up he would shop him over a job.

So tensions were running high between Ware and Everitt, each one plotting behind the other's back. This does not, however, prove that Ware intended to murder Anthony Everitt. Given a personality prone to outbursts of anger and hostility and fits of near hysteria, it may have been an impulse of the moment. Ware was certainly in a highly emotional state at the time of his arrest and again at his court appearances. At the first magistrates' hearing he broke down as the details of his arrest were given.

It was a difficult decision for the Old Bailey jury. Their verdict would depend on whether they thought Ware had intended to shoot Everitt or whether it was accidental. The judge explained in his summing up:

If . . . the jury took the view that Ware pulled out the gun in distress, and there was then a contraction of the muscles of the fingers, there would not be the intent which was required in law to establish a verdict of guilty of murder.

The jury returned a verdict of guilty of manslaughter, and the judge, describing it as 'a shocking case of manslaughter', decided that a severe custodial sentence, rather than Borstal, was required. Morris Edward Ware was sentenced to seven years in prison.

Chapter 15

A Consequence of War:
John and Rose O'Leary, 1927

The happiest couple to be found in a long day's march.

Hurrying home from morning school on Thursday two girls, Eileen, aged eleven, and her five-year-old sister, found their mother, Mrs Rose O'Leary, wife of Mr John O'Leary, dead, at 25, Cranbrook Road, Thornton Heath, and afterwards Mr O'Leary was found dead with his throat severely gashed.

his report appeared in the *Croydon Advertiser* on Saturday, 7 May 1927. In fact the younger of the two daughters, Rona, aged eight not five as reported, was the first to arrive home from Ingram Road School. Her mother had told her in the morning that she would leave a key for her in the front garden, behind some bushes. The key was not there when Rona got home at 12.30, so she went to their next-door neighbour to get the spare back door key. She called out to her mother as she opened the back door and ran through the house to the front room. There she found her mother.

Eileen returned very shortly after and a neighbour, Mrs Mary Francis, saw her crying by the front gate. She went into the house with the girls and found Rose lying on her stomach stretched out on the front room floor. The back of Rose's head was a mass of congealing blood, and a few feet from her body was a shillelagh, an Irish-style cudgel. Blood spread in a pool around her head. Taking the girls by the hands, Mrs Francis rushed out of the house to fetch PC Green, who lived next door. He had been asleep following his night shift, but had heard no commotion from his neighbours that morning.

Without stopping to investigate further at this point, and leaving Mrs Francis in charge of the crime scene, PC Green jumped on his bicycle and went to Thornton Heath Police Station to call for other officers and the police surgeon. It was only on his return to 25 Cranbrook Road that PC Green made a more extensive search of the house. In a small scullery by the coal cellar, he found John O'Leary. In PC Green's words he was

lying on his stomach, with his head near the fire grate of the copper. There was a lot of blood on the floor. His left arm was out straight

Ingram Road School (later used as military hospital). Croydon Local Studies Library

The children of Ingram Road School. Croydon Local Studies Library

and his right doubled under him. The blood was round the man's head and there was a white-handled blood-stained razor lying open on the floor near the gas stove, about five feet away from the man's head. . . . There was a large wound in the man's throat.

No one could make sense of what had happened. There was no forced entry into the house, no sign of a struggle, and no evidence of a robbery. It looked very much as though John had killed his wife, Rose, before taking his own life. The question hanging in the air was 'why?' There had been no arguments between them that anyone knew of, and neighbours described them as a devoted couple. 'They were reserved,' said one friend, 'but were excep- tionally likeable. It was easy to see that they were fond of each other and of their children, who are dear little kiddies.' John's father told the inquest that his son had never made any threats of violence whatsoever, and 'had never caused them one minute's anxiety from the day he was born'. Rose's father, George Coomber, described them as 'the happiest couple to be found in a long day's march'.

John had been working as a goods clerk for the Southern Railway Company at Waddon Station, but for about twelve weeks prior to the tragedy had been on sick leave. He was suffering from a nervous disorder and had done so since his service in the Royal Engineers in the First World War. He had seen heavy fighting in France, and like so many others had suffered from both shell- shock and a gas attack. Post-traumatic stress disorder is a familiar term to us today, but was little understood in the early part of the

Waddon Station. Croydon Local Studies Library

Waddon Station. Croydon Local Studies Library

twentieth century. It was called 'shell-shock' since it was believed to be the physiological effect on the brain of a nearby exploding shell, but it took many forms and was widely mistaken for malingering. There are a number of cases under discussion even today where men were court-martialled and even shot for deserting when, by modern standards, medical attention would have been more appropriate. A War Office investigation into shell-shock conducted in 1922 concluded that it was a genuine condition and covered a variety of neuroses.

In John O'Leary's case he suffered from severe headaches, sleeplessness and depression. The previous year he had had a serious nervous breakdown, and had been unable to work for three months. He complained of a persistent pressure on the top of his head, and although he always seemed perfectly rational, it made social interaction difficult at times. He was often seen bent over with his head in his hands. On the morning of her death, Rose had sat with her friend and neighbour, Edith Gibbons, tearfully pouring out her concerns for her husband. He had not slept properly for seven or eight weeks and Rose had been urging him to cry as a way of relieving the tension. He said he would gladly have cried all day and all night if he thought it would help. They were due to visit a doctor at a London hospital on the afternoon of their deaths, Thursday, 5 May 1927.

In the absence of any evidence to the contrary, the inquest jury was obliged to return the following verdict: 'that John O'Leary had killed his wife, afterwards committing suicide, and that he was not in his right mind when he committed these acts.'

CHAPTER 16

Death From Shock:
Mrs Eliza Ray, 1934

I may have been a bit of a rotter in my time, but I am not a liar.

It was shortly before eight o'clock in the evening and two doors from 47 Handcroft Road a dog began to howl. Its owner, Mr Smith the greengrocer, couldn't understand why the animal was so agitated. Perhaps it could hear something that he and his wife couldn't. Next door, Mrs Noone was sitting at her sewing machine, the whirring sound loud in her ears, blocking out any unusual noises that might otherwise have disturbed her.

Forty-five minutes later Mr Robert Pennefather returned to the house from his customary stroll into Croydon town centre. He was in the habit of spending half an hour or so each evening with his friend Mr Schulman, the tailor, and this evening was no exception. As a retired Warrant Officer of the Royal Air Force he was a man of regular habits. At 8.35 he let himself in to 47 Handcroft Road where he lodged in the home of Mrs Eliza Ray, and was surprised to see the hall rugs strewn untidily across the floor and the outer bolt drawn on the door to the back room. The door was usually left open so that the light could shine through to illuminate the hallway, and he was puzzled to see it locked. Suspecting something was amiss he slid back the bolt, opened the door and took in the gaslit scene before him. He barely noticed the ransacked room – all he saw was seventy-six-year-old Mrs Ray stretched out on the floor, her feet pointing towards the window, and a cloth carefully laid over her face.

Shocked, he rushed into the

47 Handcroft Road, 1934. Croydon Local Studies Library

Mr Robert Pennefather with Mrs Chamberlain, Eliza Ray's daughter.
Croydon Local Studies Library

street shouting, 'She's dead; she's been murdered.'

He turned first to his neighbour, Mrs Lilian Arch, and together they went back into the house. Tentatively Mrs Arch touched Eliza Ray's arm; it was cold. Mr Pennefather urged her to remove the cloth from the old lady's face but she was too afraid. Instead, she suggested, they should inform the police. Mr Pennefather returned to the street in search of a constable, while Mrs Arch rushed to Sutherland Road, to the home of Mrs Chamberlain, one of Eliza's three daughters.

It was February 1934, a time when police on the beat were easily found, and PC John Stinchcombe happened to be walking along Handcroft Road. He went to number 47 with Mr Pennefather and together they examined the downstairs rooms, all of which were in a state of disarray. Drawers had been left open and their contents strewn about, a writing desk broken into, even Mrs Ray's purse had been upturned and all but emptied of money. The police officer removed the cloth from Eliza Ray's face. There were several bruises and some blood; a handkerchief had been tied tightly round her mouth. When this was later removed they saw that another cloth had been pushed into her mouth with such force that it reached down into her throat and her upper dentures had been rammed to the back of her mouth.

Within fifteen minutes the usually quiet road was abuzz with police cars and an ambulance. Well into the early hours of the following morning, detectives from Scotland Yard were at work searching for fingerprints and taking photographs of the crime scene by flashlight.

According to the *Croydon Times* police were able to reconstruct at least some of the events of that evening. 'It appears', they reported, 'that Mrs Ray was attacked in the hall, where there were signs of a struggle, knocked unconscious, dragged into the living

Mrs Eliza Ray. Croydon Local Studies Library

room, gagged and left to die while the murderer carried out his search for valuables.'

A sense of panic spread through the neighbourhood. By morning crowds of people had gathered in Handcroft Road in search of information and reassurance. Was the murderer like to strike again, they wanted to know. Eliza Ray's body was removed to the Mayday Mortuary where a post-mortem examination concluded that she had died of 'shock due to partial asphyxiation as a result of external pressure'. The hunt for the murderer was on.

Neighbours were interviewed: no one had heard anything but they knew that Mrs Ray was always very cautious about opening the door to strangers. She would have put up a fight despite her age. And, they recalled, there were similarities between this murder and one that had hit the headlines two years earlier. Then, a housekeeper, Miss Susannah Emberton, had been attacked and left to die of her injuries while the assailant ransacked the house of her employer, Mr Ells Dagnell, in search of valuables. No one had ever been arrested for Miss Emberton's murder.

Now, in the words of the *Croydon Advertiser*, the police 'carried out an exhaustive comb-out'. They made door-to-door inquiries, searched lodging houses, pawnbrokers and second-hand shops; they took known local criminals to Croydon Police Station for questioning. As a result of this they were able to match a finger-print from 47 Handcroft Road to a name that had cropped up during their inquiries – that of thirty-two-year-old Leslie Martin.

Crowds gathered at the Magistrates' Court to see Martin charged with the murder of Eliza Ray. He was of slight build with fair, curly hair, and he leaned over the rail in front of him so that he could take in every detail of the proceedings. His profession was described as 'motor driver' and his residence was given as Mitcham Road, Croydon. He claimed to be 'perfectly innocent'.

But between the remand hearing and the magistrates' hearing, two further arrests were made. They were of twenty-nine-year-old

Surrey Street, Croydon. Croydon Local Studies Library

Albert Ansell, a printer's cutter from Kennington, and twenty-four-year-old Walter Ross, a leather stainer from Camberwell. The two men had been drinking with Martin in the *Derby Arms* public house on the evening of the murder and further evidence came to light that linked them to the crime. All was revealed at their trial at the Old Bailey in March that year.

The key witness was Mr William Knowles, a street trader in Surrey Street who, like Mrs Ray, lived in Handcroft Road. On the Wednesday before the murder he had met with Leslie Martin at the *Britannia* public house and later that evening they moved on to the *Cannon*. Martin was complaining about a shortage of money and Knowles told him that there were thousands of pounds to be had in Croydon. Martin was interested to know where, but Knowles said he merely teased Martin with the reply, 'Find out.' On their walk between pubs they met several acquaintances, including Mr Schulman, the friend of Eliza Ray's lodger. Schulman and Martin chatted alone for a while. When William Knowles and Leslie Martin passed along Handcroft Road, Martin pointed out number 47 and said to Knowles, 'That's the house that Schulman told me about.' It was apparently known that Mrs Ray received an income from the rent on a property left to her by her parents. It was thought that she kept the money in her house. Mr Pennefather confirmed that he regularly cashed the rental cheques locally on her behalf , and although he had no reason to believe that Eliza Ray kept any large amounts of money in the house, the rumour was about, and that was enough to set off the train of events that ended in her death.

William Knowles made it seem as though all the information about Mrs Ray's money had come from Mr Schulman, the tailor. In fact Knowles was far more deeply involved in the affair than he cared to admit, as Leslie Martin revealed when he finally gave a full statement to the police. It was Knowles who had told him about the money, an estimated £3,000; he had said that it could be found in the drawer of a chiffonier in the bedroom and he also suggested various ways they might go about the job. Because the lodger, Mr Pennefather, went out each evening with such precise regularity, it would be easy to catch Eliza Ray alone in the house. They could force their way in once she opened the door, he suggested, or take a ladder and climb up to the bedroom window. He expected a share of the takings. Mr Schulman did nothing more than confirm the information that he'd learned from his friend, Robert Pennefather.

The police statements of the key players in this drama make interesting reading. They are all eager to point the finger of blame at the others and to claim their own innocence. Knowles admitted he told Martin that there was money to be had, but initially denied that detailed information ever came from him. In his version of events Martin took the leading role in the crime. On the afternoon of Saturday, 17 February 1934 Martin told him that they (he and two friends) were 'going to do that show tonight', and later that evening that 'we turned that rat over and we never found anything – not a light.' Knowles claimed he had wanted reassurance that they hadn't hurt Mrs Ray, and Martin said they had done nothing

Cannon Inn *public house, Handcroft Road.* Croydon Local Studies Library

other than push her in the kitchen. When Knowles became alarmed at the sight of the ambulance, all Martin said was, 'You'll know all about it in a minute.' As the news of the death became known, Knowles claimed to have been deeply angry and said that he'd accused Martin of being 'a murdering bastard'.

In Leslie Martin's version of events Knowles was the source of all information, and discussed openly how the job could best be carried out. But Martin was reluctant to do the deed himself as he was well known in the area and would be one of the first suspects for the police. Instead, he said, he passed the information on to Ansell and Ross, introduced them to Knowles and waited in the street while they carried out the burglary. When no money was found, he was concerned that Knowles would think they were trying to cheat him out of his share of the booty and insisted that Ansell and Ross explain the situation personally to Knowles. He denied that Knowles had called him a murdering bastard.

Ansell and Ross had clearly worked out their stories together. They both refer to Leslie Martin as either 'Curly' or 'Fairy' Jones (Martin used several different surnames at different points in his life). The two men admitted being with Martin in the *Derby* public house on the night of the murder. Ross played darts with 'Curly' while Ansell watched. They left the pub at ten minutes to eight and caught two buses back to the Carter Street Billiards Club in Walworth where they played pool for most of the night. Leslie Martin joined them at the billiards hall between 11.30 and

Funeral of Eliza Ray. Croydon Local Studies Library

midnight, but they knew nothing of the burglary or the death of Mrs Ray until they read of it in the papers. They stuck fast to their story.

Knowles's testimony was damaging to all three men, and the fingerprint that placed Leslie Martin at the scene of the crime destroyed his claim that he had merely waited outside while Ansell and Ross carried out the burglary alone. Despite their statements it was evident that all three men were involved, and this was confirmed by another witness.

Cyril Geoffrey Harris was in Brixton Prison awaiting trial on a charge of indecent assault. In that time he got to know Ross, who was awaiting his own trial at the Old Bailey. Harris recalled one occasion when a group of men, including himself and Ross, sat round a fire discussing the difference between murder and manslaughter. Harris decided to use the case of Eliza Ray to illustrate the point. 'To give you an example,' he said, pointing a finger at Ross, 'you struck the woman, she fell to the ground and although she did not die the moment she went to the floor, it would be murder just the same.' Ross reddened in the face. The two men discussed the matter again when they were alone, and Harris commented on the way Ross had blushed. Ross started to deny that he'd had anything to do with the murder, but eventually opened up:

> *I tell you what happened. We thought there was more than there was in the place. . . . We got in the house. I held the woman and Martin gagged her. Ansell took a look round the house.*

After their trial in April 1934 all three men were found guilty and sentenced to be hanged. The scene in court was emotionally charged and was reported in dramatic detail by the *Croydon Times*:

> *The usher calls for silence under penalty of imprisonment, but already there is a silence which can almost be felt. The three prisoners stand mute and dazed. The Judge, with a hand that can be seen to shake, adjusts the black cap, and from a hidden corner in the Court his chaplain glides noiselessly to his place behind the Judge's chair. . . . Martin clings to the dock rails, a stuttering noise comes from his lips and then in a burst: 'I may have been a bit of a rotter in my time, but I am not a liar.' . . . Ross gives a pathetic wave to a woman in the back of the Court, a low wail echoes round the Court and the dock is empty. Outside in the corridor sat three inconsolable women, covering their eyes as if to shut out the memory of that dreadful scene when their husbands were sent to the brink of*

Eternity and told that the law would demand an expiation of their crime by death.

They all three lodged appeals, which in the cases of Walter Ross and Albert Ansell were allowed; the judgement against them was quashed and they were acquitted, presumably because of the lack of physical evidence against them. Leslie Martin's appeal was denied, but in June that same year, and following a vigorous campaign by his wife, his sentence was commuted to penal servitude for life just twenty-four hours before the death sentence was due to be carried out.

The irony of the case was that although Mrs Ray did not keep large sums of money in her house, her jewellery and more than £14 remained untouched in the one drawer of the chiffonier that Ansell did not open. The drawer was locked, it is true, but the key to it sat in the bottom of the next drawer. He had been in such a hurry that the only money they got away with came from her purse in the drawing room. Eliza Ray had died for 3 shillings and sixpence.

CHAPTER 17

Dangerous When Alone: Gilbert Wright, 1895

Come home at once. I have settled Bertie and I have gone to the station.

The Wright family was well respected within the community in Thornton Heath. David Wright worked hard as a foreman clerk for the London, Brighton and South Coast Railway Company, at Norwood Junction, and his sixteen-year-old son Jesse worked for the same company. An older brother, Andrew, was independently established. Charlotte Wright kept a neat and tidy house and the younger children, Lottie, aged twelve, and Gilbert, known to the family as Bertie, were always loved and well cared for. Neighbours saw the Wright family as 'a singularly united and happy one', although not every member of the family was quite as happy as they seemed.

On Tuesday, 29 October 1895 they breakfasted together at their home in Pawson Road, Thornton Heath. Jesse had just returned from the night shift and joined the rest of the family for breakfast before getting some sleep. His mother ate a little bread and butter and drank some tea, but everyone could see that she seemed to be in very low spirits. This was not unusual – in recent

Norwood Junction Station, where both David Wright and his son Jesse worked.
Croydon Local Studies Library

Lottie's school at Princess Road. Croydon Local Studies Library

months she had struggled with frequent bouts of depression.

Charlotte had wanted Lottie to stay home from school. She needed her to run some errands, she said, but Lottie wasn't happy about this. She was a bright, articulate child who enjoyed school, and was especially keen to attend that day as she had been chosen to take part in a cookery competition. Bertie, on the other hand, was only seven years old and had very little say in the matter. His mother decided that he should stay at home and no one said anything to try to change her mind. So Bertie accompanied his father on the first leg of his walk to work, then kissed him goodbye before running back home to his mother. It was a kiss that David Wright would have cause to remember.

Lottie walked to the Princess Road Board School on her own that morning, anticipating the day's activities. At noon she was surprised to learn that her mother had come to the school, just as Lottie's class was in the middle of a test.

Mrs Wright asked for permission to speak to her daughter. A governess explained that that would not be possible because the class was in the middle of an examination, but Charlotte Wright, usually such a mild-mannered woman, insisted most forcefully. She needed to speak to her daughter.

Lottie was allowed a few moments with her mother in the school porch. There Mrs Wright handed her a key to the house and a folded note that she was to take to her father as soon as possible. With a kiss and a hug she reminded Lottie to be a good girl and left, telling her that Bertie was at home. Charlotte Wright seemed calm but purposeful – there was no sign that she had been crying.

Instead of simply delivering the note to her father as instructed, Lottie unfolded the piece of paper and read what her mother had written:

> *Dave – Come home at once. I have settled Bertie and I have gone to the station. I trust you will be as kind as you can to the children, and I hope that you and Rachel will make your home together. Try for Fan and Kate to have Lottie. – From your wife.*

Then underneath, on the same piece of paper:

> *Dearest Rachel – Do your best for Dave. He is a good man. I have had this in my head for months. I tried twice to commit suicide.*

Rachel was David Wright's sister, and Fan and Kate were sisters of Charlotte Wright.

Lottie failed to grasp the implication of the note. She didn't like the idea of leaving Bertie at home on his own, so before she did anything else she went to Pawson Road to collect him; they could take the note to their father together, she thought. And so it was Lottie who discovered exactly what her mother had meant by 'I have settled Bertie.' The *Croydon Times* described what she found:

> *When she got inside the kitchen she saw something lying under a cover – a table cover. She lifted up the cloth and found Bertie lying beneath it. He was fully dressed and was lying a little on one side. His hands and feet were bound, the latter by the ankles. A scarf was round his feet (Bertie usually wore the scarf . . .) and a black waistband was round his wrists. A piece of rope was twisted round his neck, and his face had a blackish appearance. There was some blood, which had come from his nose.*

It is hard to imagine what Lottie must have felt. She ran to her father at work, thrust her mother's note into his hands, and spilled out her dreadful story as they both rushed back home. As they neared the house they met a police officer, PC William Harvey, and asked him to go inside with them. David Wright found the scene exactly as Lottie had described it; he must have been hoping against hope that she had been mistaken.

PC Harvey and David Wright lifted Bertie onto the kitchen table, and tried to revive him with artificial respiration. They continued their efforts until the arrival of Dr Robert Fleming, who took over from them. Bertie's body was still warm, but there was no pulse. After fifteen minutes the doctor reluctantly admitted defeat and all efforts to revive Bertie were stopped. He was then able to examine the body for injuries. He told the inquest jury:

> *I found two circular marks round the neck, depressed as if by ligatures, and with an effusion of blood under them, beneath the skin. The face was livid and swollen, and the pupils of the eyes were both dilated and swollen. A little blood was coming from the nostrils and the fingers were clenched.*

There was no sign of Charlotte Wright. Jesse was still asleep upstairs – there had been no screams and no sounds of a struggle to wake him. PC O'Brien, Detective Sergeant Stemp and David Wright set out to find Charlotte, more than half expecting her to have killed herself. In fact, arrangements were being made to drag the gravel pits in Thornton Heath when they found her. She was in the High Street, near the top of Crown Hill, looking for the police station. The station had recently been moved from North End, and Charlotte looked lost and bewildered.

She was arrested and in reply said simply, 'Bertie? Yes I did

North End by Crown Hill, where Charlotte was found looking for the police station. Croydon Local Studies Library

murder him.' Back at the police station she was formally charged with 'killing and slaying' her son. The wording of the charge distressed her. 'What is "killing and slaying"?' she asked. 'I did not cut him.'

Charlotte's family, friends and even her doctor had known her to be in a depressed state for some months, but no one had appreciated the depth of her anguish. She had been fighting hard to control her emotions, and the strain of keeping her home in good order and her family well cared for was becoming more and more difficult to bear. She confided in a friend, Catherine Durman, who also lived in Pawson Road, that she felt very ill indeed and suffered from pains in her head and sleeplessness. She also told Mrs Durman, 'I feel dangerous when I am alone, and at times I am afraid to be alone.' Her friend advised her to get out for a change of air, but with so many meals to prepare and the house to clean Charlotte did not feel this was possible.

At the time of her arrest Charlotte was finding it hard to comprehend the reality of her situation. But at the magistrates' hearing and again at her trial at the Central Criminal Court, Charlotte was obliged to listen to all the details of her desperate act. Throughout her court appearances she kept her face buried in her arms or her hands, and wept continuously, mostly in silence. But when the details of Bertie's death were presented to the Court, she cried in audible sobs.

Exactly why she murdered her son was never clarified. Perhaps it was beyond even her own understanding, so deep was her depression. But how she did it was explained. Bertie was a large boy for his age, and strong. Charlotte, on the other hand, had been weakened by months of illness. Although Bertie was only seven years old, she would have found it very difficult to bind his hands and feet against his will. And so she made a game of it, 'a romp' in her words. The little boy giggled with anticipation as his normally caring and loving mother tied him up, and he waited for the fun to begin. But his laughter must have turned to bewilderment and then fear as she tied a piece of clothes line around his neck. 'What have I done, Mammy?' he asked her, 'what have I done?' She tightened the rope, tied it as firmly as she could and then covered his body with a table cloth.

At her trial and in the press much was made of the imbalance of a woman's mind at the time of the menopause. A Dr Fowler, under examination at the Old Bailey trial, told the Court that 'the change of life did sometimes occasion insanity', and that this was 'a very dangerous period' for a woman. She was referred to as a 'demented mother', and the *Croydon Review* commented that 'there is no question that the poor woman was out of her mind, a condition arising from various causes, chief of which probably was the lasting housework incidental to the preparation of meals for the family.' Clinical depression, rather than too much housework, would be a more obvious diagnosis today.

It was impossible not to sympathize with a woman who was so deeply disturbed, however distasteful her actions had been. The judge, in his summing up of the case, felt that Charlotte Wright, though guilty in the eyes of the law, should be exonerated from moral blame. The jury agreed. They were obliged to find her guilty, but pronounced her not responsible for her own actions. She was ordered to be detained during Her Majesty's pleasure.

Bertie's funeral was as sad as might be expected. There was no hearse: the small coffin travelled in the carriage with his father and brothers. So many people pressed around the graveside that police were required to hold the crowds back for fear of an accident. But everyone wanted to express their sympathy, some even for the mother who had caused so much misery.

CHAPTER 18

Kiss of Death:
Carol Ann Soan, 1959

*They were very much in love with each other and went out
hand-in-hand.*

The couple stood close together, facing each other, deep
in conversation – a vignette of young love taking advan-
tage of the solitude and privacy of Norwood Grove
Recreation Ground. It was about ten o'clock in the
evening and no one was around to disturb them. The girl, no
more than seventeen years of age, leaned forward to kiss the man,
her senior by five years, and for a moment they remained motion-
less, his hand cupping the back of her head. Then as they kissed,
he moved his hands down to her neck and on to her throat, and
began to squeeze. She made some strange, throaty sounds as she
dropped to her knees, but he knelt with her, keeping his grip as
firm as ever. Again the pose was held for a moment or two until
he reached into his pocket for a length of cord, which he tied very
tightly round her neck, fastening it with a reef knot to the side.

It was February 1959 and Eddie Barber was happy with his lot

Norwood Grove. Croydon Local Studies Library

in life. The main source of this happiness was his engagement to seventeen-year-old Carol Soan. They had decided to marry the previous year and worked out that it would take them just one more year to save the £500 they felt they needed to set up home together. Carol was saving hard, putting away the money she earned in different envelopes so that she could pay her fares to work, her mother for her board and keep, and then save as much as possible. Eddie did likewise with his wages as a bread packer and in this way they'd already managed to save £150.

Although Eddie was twenty-two years old, Carol was his first girlfriend and she rapidly became the focus of his entire world. He was gentle with her and generally easygoing, though they had their tiffs like anyone else.

Carol was a shorthand typist and lived with her family in Hawthorn Avenue, Thornton Heath. She lived quietly and was generally thought of as a 'sweet girl' by those who knew her. Her parents, Josephine and John, approved of her engagement to Eddie, and welcomed him into their home as a son.

On 25 February 1959 Eddie called for Carol at her home. After just fifteen minutes they left together. Later Carol's father remarked that they were 'very much in love with each other and went out hand-in-hand'. They had no elaborate plans for the evening, but intended simply to go back to Eddie's home in Virginia Road, Thornton Heath, to watch the television. They sat together in the front room of his parents' house while his mother pottered in the kitchen and his father remained upstairs in the bedroom. There had been a few minor arguments between them recently – nothing serious, and mostly over such trivial things as what they were going to watch on the television. Then Carol dropped her bombshell. She wanted to end the relationship, she said. She'd met someone at work, a man who worked at the same office, and she couldn't get him out of her mind. She said she felt it would be better for both of them. His parents heard him cry out, 'No, no, Carol, not that!' And then he broke down and sobbed openly.

Eddie's parents then came in and did what they could to console him. His mother offered the advice that if Carol wanted to leave him, there was nothing he could do to stop her and that he should try to come to terms with the situation. She knew how upsetting it must be, but all they could do was talk it over together. She advised him to take Carol home, and try to talk the matter out as they walked. But Eddie was so emotionally overwrought that he found it hard to think rationally. He took a knife from the kitchen and hid it in his pocket, resolving that if they could not work things out he would end his own life.

They walked as far as Streatham Common, Eddie pleading with Carol to change her mind. She remained adamant. They turned and headed back towards Carol's home and stopped at Norwood Grove, just a short way from the footpath. Eddie asked her to kiss him one last time and his hands closed around her throat.

As Carol fell to her knees Eddie became panic-stricken. He was afraid she would cry out and he was afraid he had hurt her; he couldn't decide whether it would be worse for her if he loosened his grip on her throat and left her dying in pain, or whether he should try to finish her off as quickly as possible. His solution was to take the cord that he regularly used to tie round his jacket while he was working, and tie it as tightly as possible round her neck to end her suffering. In his words:

She went down and murmured a bit, I thought if I let her go she would scream. I didn't know whether to let her go or squeeze more. She was making some funny noises, breathing noises you know, it frightened me a bit so I got the rope out of my pocket, tied it round her neck, I was frightened to let go, I didn't want her to be in agony. I took the knife from my pocket and tossed it by the tree. I wouldn't have dreamed of using it on her. She didn't move and I came away.

Eddie walked to the telephone box on Green Lane and dialled 999. He asked the police to come to his home at 21 Virginia Road, and waited on the corner of the street for them to arrive. When he saw the police car he flagged it down and said, 'I think I have killed my girlfriend. You'll find her body in the grove.'

Edmund William Charles Barber was arrested for the self-confessed murder of Carol Ann Soan. He was first interviewed by the police at his parents' house and then accompanied them to Norwood Grove where her body still lay. Eddie stayed in the police car while the officers went to examine the crime scene. PC Bernard Holmes tried to remove the cord from around Carol's neck, but the task proved difficult as the ligature was now deeply embedded in her flesh. When he returned to the car, Eddie asked him, 'Can you tell me if the girl is dead?' In reality he did not need to be told the answer to his question – it was more in the nature of a forlorn hope.

Over the coming weeks Eddie underwent in-depth psychiatric evaluation. The Principal Medical Officer of Brixton Prison, F H Brisby, was very struck by several aspects of his interviews with Eddie. First, that he appeared somewhat detached when he spoke about the murder, more as though he had been a witness rather than a participant in the crime. 'He fails to appreciate the enormity of the whole occurrence, yet he is not a callous type but appears so far as I can judge to be of benign personality.' Second, he felt that 'this man talked and acted rather under his years and I formed the opinion that he was of sub-average intelligence and a simple immature type.' However, subsequent psychometric testing showed that Edmund Barber was in fact of slightly above average intelligence, suggesting that his problem was one of extreme emotional immaturity rather than deficiency of intellect. In the words of Dr Brisby, 'It would not, in my opinion, be over-stating it to say that emotionally he is just a big unsophisticated schoolboy,' and that this emotional immaturity, when combined with an above-average intelligence 'suggests a mentality verging on the pathological'.

There was one dark incident from Eddie's past that came to light in the course of the interviews, and that centred around an attempt to take his own life while in the army. Following a bout of depression, caused in Eddie's view by the gloomy atmosphere at the Tower of London where he was serving, he slit his wrists and made his way back to his mother in Croydon. Mrs Barber took him immediately to the Mayday Hospital for stitches and he was placed under psychiatric care. Eddie's military career was short-lived as a result of this.

In spite of this history, Eddie was deemed fit to stand trial. As the sad events unfolded before both the jury and the attendant press reporters, it was difficult not to feel sympathy for this man,

Mayday Hospital, 1959. Mrs Barber took Eddie for treatment here following his suicide attempt. Croydon Local Studies Library

even in the face of his dreadful crime. After a period of just eighty-one minutes the jury returned a verdict of not guilty to the charge of murder, but guilty of manslaughter. In sentencing him the judge, Mr Justice Elwes, promised to show as much mercy as possible, but felt compelled, at the same time, to deal with the serious nature of the crime. Edmund Barber was sentenced to three years in prison.

In cases of murder it is often easy to feel overwhelmed by the darker side of human nature. But occasionally one encounters an example of simple kindness that is truly uplifting. And out of the sadness that enveloped the protagonists of this history emerged one such example. Just three days after the devastating loss of her daughter, Carol's mother, Josephine, wrote to Eddie in prison, demonstrating the most remarkable compassion and magnanimity.

Our Dear Son Eddie

John and I have just been to see Mum and Dad Barber. They told us you would like us to write to you. We do not want you to reproach yourself about this unfortunate tragedy. We know how much you have been suffering at this time. Our thoughts are always with you. When you come home you will have as warm a welcome as if you were our own boy . . . No one can find it in their hearts to blame you. We will do everything in our power to help you, so please Eddie keep your chin up. All the children send their love and we send our fondest love and sympathy.

Mum and Dad Soan

Mustard and Cress Murder: Mary Carver, 1870

We should advise Mr Carver never to come near Croydon again.

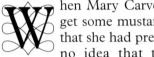hen Mary Carver went to her next-door neighbour to get some mustard and cress to go with the boiled ham that she had prepared for her husband's lunch, she had no idea that the meal would end in her death. Arguments always have two sides, but we have just a few scraps of information to build up Mary's version of the quarrel.

Mary lived with her husband, John, their one-year-old child and a domestic servant at 35 South End, Croydon. John worked as an upholsterer and ran his shop from the house. Sharing the premises was the Morgan family, who ran their building company from their side of the house. The story of what happened on 26 May 1870 comes principally from John Carver's lips.

John came home rather later than usual for lunch that day. He arrived at two o'clock and Mary suspected that the delay might have been caused by a visit to the *Surrey Drovers* public house; according to John she was not happy about having to wait for her

South End, home of the Carver family. Croydon Local Studies Library

The Surrey Drovers *public house, where Mary suspected John had stopped to drink.* Croydon Local Studies Library

meal. He asked her to get some mustard and cress from Mrs Morgan, and this Mary did. When she returned John cut some and gave it to his wife to wash. She came back to the table and put the cress down on the first of three plates sitting in a pile on the table. What she probably didn't realize was that the top plate had already been used by their servant girl. Mary had put the mustard and cress on a dirty plate and the clean ones sat beneath it. It seems a small transgression, and most likely accidental, but it sent John into a rage. He picked up the plates and threw them against the wall, smashing them. He then picked up the carving knife, and in his version of events, continued carving the ham. He had the carving knife and fork in his hands when it was Mary's turn to get angry. She rushed at him, he said, knocking him backwards over his chair until he found himself pinned awkwardly against the wall, his elbows bent to steady himself, and the knife and fork sticking out in front of him. The carving knife slid into Mary, penetrating about four inches to cause a wound just above her left breast. John claims not to have realized what had happened.

She walked back to her chair at the table, before dropping to the floor. John thought she had fainted, and then that perhaps she was having a fit, since this had happened before. But no. He saw the scarlet stain spread across her bodice and ran to Mrs Morgan for help.

'Will you send for Dr Cole,' he called to his neighbour, 'I think Mrs Carver is dead.'

'Never!' said Mrs Morgan in disbelief, as she followed John into the back parlour. There she saw Mary Carver on the floor, and her first instinct was to fetch some vinegar to bathe Mary's head, as she did not truly believe her to be dead. But she soon realized that it was true.

'Oh you wretch!' was all she could say to John, as she had over-heard him calling Mary 'a dirty bitch' just moments earlier and assumed that he had killed her in the course of an argument. She had overheard more than one in her time.

'It's an accident,' John told her.

The servant girl was sent to bring back Dr Cole and, at John's request, Mrs Morgan went to fetch the police. They soon arrived and took full statements from both John Carver and Mrs Morgan. John was duly arrested for his wife's murder. Within hours, news of the death had spread throughout the neighbourhood.

Crowds filled both the streets and the courtroom on the day of the magistrates' hearing. John retold his story, as did Mrs Morgan and the attending police officers. One additional witness gave interesting, if slightly suspect, evidence. George Miller, landlord of the *Purley Arms* public house, said that he looked into John Carver's shop between half past two and three o'clock on the afternoon of the murder, as he was looking for a bath chair for his wife and wondered if Mr Carver had one in his shop. As he stood by the shop door, he said,

I heard a man's voice in the little back parlour behind the shop say, 'I will smash your b— brains out.' Then I saw the prisoner pass the glass panels of the door . . . I saw him stoop or fall down, and while in that position he raised his arm three or four times in quick succession. His hand appeared closed. The action appeared as blows given.

The image of a shadowy figure raising his arm to strike some-thing beneath him three times might have come straight from the pages of a Victorian penny-dreadful novel. But there was only one wound to Mary Carver, a single clean and deep wound above her breast. That does cast doubt over George Miller's evidence, but at the same time his words give some colour to John's anger, at least in terms of his shouting threatening words at his wife. Both George Miller and Mary Ann Morgan had heard John Carver shouting aggressive and abusive words at his wife. They both say they heard not a single word in reply from her.

The young girl who worked as a servant to the Carvers was not

Shop in South End established in the year of Mary's death. It was just a few doors from the Carvers' home.
Croydon Local Studies Library

present at the time of the death and therefore had little evidence to give. But she did point out that about an hour before the incident she had gone into the house to get some water, and found Mary Carver sitting in a chair, crying. There was no obvious cause for tears, but neighbours had heard the couple arguing in the morning for about an hour. It was generally felt, however, that John and Mary Carver 'were very fond of each other'.

John Carver listened carefully to the evidence given by the witnesses, and challenged one or two of the statements made. PC Thomas Floyd, a young and relatively inexperienced officer, was the first on the scene. He told the court that Carver explained what had happened, using the phrases, 'I've killed her; it's quite an accident,' and later on, 'This is the knife I killed her with.' Carver denied that he had ever said, 'I killed her,' but claimed he'd said instead, 'She's dead, she's done it herself, because she ran against the knife herself.' The police officer restated his conviction that Carver had used the words, 'I killed her.'

The *Croydon Advertiser* painted an interesting word picture of John Carver in the prisoner's box:

> *He is a moderately-built man, only about five feet six inches in height. There is nothing vicious or striking in his features, which are rather dark, and appear slightly swollen as if he were accustomed to drink. He has only one child, but it is said he has been married more than once, the woman now lying dead being about five years his junior.*

John asked the court for permission to see his wife one last time, a request that speaks of emotions that lay deeper than his periodic outbursts of anger. He was taken from the Magistrates' Court to Horsemonger Lane Gaol, looking 'very pale and care-worn' through streets lined with onlookers demonstrating their disapproval. He was to be held on remand, awaiting a hearing at the County Assizes in August.

The inquest into Mary Carver's death returned a verdict not of accidental death, but of 'wilful murder against John Carver'. The inquest jury was unanimous.

When he appeared at the assizes the *Croydon Advertiser* reported that Carver seemed 'exceedingly depressed and showed intimations of mental anguish'. The evidence was in essence the same as at the magistrates' hearing, but with special weight now being placed by the prosecution on the evidence of George Miller, the pub landlord who claimed to have seen Carver through the window of his shop raising his arm above his head and lowering it three or four times in quick succession, as though striking at a person or an object on the floor.

Both prosecuting and defence counsel put forward eloquent and persuasive arguments. Mr Lilley, for the prosecution, tried to throw serious doubt on Carver's version of events. He argued:

> *If there was great impulsiveness, and a person was of considerable weight, such an accident might occur; but it would be proved that Mrs Carver was only about 5ft and 3ins in height, and was not a stout or heavy woman, and it was for the jury to say whether it was reasonable that such a stab could be received as the prisoner stated with an ordinary table knife.*

The defence countered with an emotional speech. It was 'a very sad and lamentable accident', Mr Sergeant Sleigh said, 'which the prisoner must deplore to the very latest day of his life'. But, he contended, the physical evidence of Mrs Carver's injury was entirely in keeping with the version of events put forward by the accused.

Everyone expected an acquittal; the courtroom was shocked into momentary silence therefore, by the jury's verdict of 'guilty of wilful murder', but delivered with a strong recommendation for mercy.

The *Croydon Advertiser* reported that John Carver had behaved throughout the trial with 'a dignified calmness'. Nonetheless, he betrayed, they said, 'intense emotion, when, shortly before sentence of death was passed on him, he alluded to his affection for his wife and his preparation for death'.

The truth of whether John Carver played an active part in his wife's death will remain a mystery. Did he pull her body onto the knife as he held it outstretched in his hand? Did he stab her while she lay on the floor, as suggested by George Miller's evidence? Or did she run onto the knife in a fit of rage, as the prisoner claimed?

It is impossible to know with any certainty. But we do know what happened to John Carver. Immediately after the trial his solicitor, Mr H Parry, wrote to the Home Secretary requesting not just mercy, but a full pardon. Surprisingly, and for reasons that have been lost to us, this was granted within a few weeks, and John Carver was given his freedom. However, the general public has a mind of its own, and when he returned home to retrieve some possessions, he was greeted by a mob, some there to congratulate him on his release, others with less generous motives. He was forced to take refuge in a nearby public house, and await a police escort to see him safely out of the area. The *Croydon Advertiser* summed up the situation:

> *Mob law is not always justice; but it appears that the elderly ladies of South End and the Home Secretary are greatly at variance on the subject of Carver's incarceration and pardon. We should advise Mr Carver never to come near Croydon again, however much his feelings may be hurt by such an involuntary exile.*

CHAPTER 20

The Curious Mr Brinkley: Richard and Anne Beck, 1907

Well I'm sugared. This is very awkward, isn't it?

Richard Brinkley was shocked to be arrested for the murders of Richard and Anne Beck. He had met Richard Beck only once, and then but briefly, and he had never met Anne Beck at all. 'Well I'm sugared,' he said to the arresting officer, Detective Inspector Fowler. 'Well I'm sugared. This is very awkward, isn't it?'

The previous day, Saturday, 20 April 1907, Richard Brinkley had visited, by appointment, a man named Reginald Parker. Mr Parker was an accountant, and the two men had had certain business dealings in the past when Brinkley needed documents or letters written for him. A carpenter by trade, Brinkley claimed he was not good at letter writing. But this particular meeting had nothing to do with business – it was about the purchase of a dog. Brinkley needed a dog to guard a property he had inherited, and knew that Reginald Parker had good contacts and would be able to find a nicely vicious bulldog, or something similar, for him.

The meeting took place at 32 Churchill Road, Croydon, at the home of Richard and Anne Beck. This was where Reginald Parker had recently rented a room, following his separation from his wife. And the Becks showed every sign of being friendly and considerate landlords: Richard Beck was always willing to have a companionable drink with his new tenant, or light a fire for him when he was due to come home, and Mrs Beck was happy to have a hot meal ready.

In fact when Richard Brinkley arrived at Churchill Road, Reginald Parker and Richard Beck were chatting over a bottle of ale in the living room, and they invited the visitor to join them. With a flourish, Brinkley produced a bottle of oatmeal stout from his pocket and said he would be glad to. This was perhaps a little odd for a confirmed teetotaller – one, moreover, who took his convictions to the point of joining his local division of the Sons of Temperance. But, he explained, his doctor had recently advised him to drink stout. He drank a little oatmeal stout from his glass, poured a glass for Reginald Parker, who also drank some, and put the rest of the bottle to one side. Mr Beck left the other two men alone to conduct their negotiations about the bulldog, which

Brighton Road, South Croydon in 1907. Croydon Local Studies Library

Brinkley decided to buy for £5, and arrangements were made for Parker to take the dog to Brinkley's home in Fulham on the following morning. Brinkley then asked Reginald Parker for a glass of water, and he was alone in the room for less than one minute while Parker went to fetch it.

Richard Brinkley drank his water and left the house in Churchill Road with Reginald Parker, who had plans to stay with a friend in Brighton Road that night. The bottle of stout remained in the living room.

Reginald Parker was woken by the arrival of the police at the home of his friend in Brighton Road. Without ceremony they walked into his bedroom, shining a light in his face and asking what he knew about Richard and Anne Beck. They had been found dying, he was informed, when the police were called to Churchill Road in the early hours of the morning. Dr William Dempster was already in attendance, but Richard and Anne were by this time unconscious on the kitchen floor and there was nothing the doctor could do for them. They died shortly after. Their daughter, Daisy, was lying on the couch, barely conscious, and she was taken to Croydon Hospital where doctors were able to save her life.

In Dr Dempster's opinion they had all been poisoned. There was a very distinctive smell, and although the doctor at first

Croydon General Hospital, where Daisy Beck's life was saved. Croydon Local Studies Library

believed it to be cyanide of potassium, it turned out to be prussic acid. And the same recognizable smell came from the bottle of oatmeal stout.

Reginald Parker told the police everything that had happened the night before, and at midnight on the Sunday Richard Brinkley was arrested at his home for murder. He denied everything; he even denied ever having visited Croydon and said that he had not seen Reginald Parker for at least three weeks. He was appalled at the thought of being held in the cells overnight and when he was forced to face the reality of his situation, he became agitated. Either he was lying or Reginald Parker was, and Brinkley did everything to convince the police of his respectability. He first of all asked permission to send word to his Masonic lodge, then reminded them that he was a teetotaller and of established good character. 'Does Parker say I done it?' he asked. 'He is a dirty tyke, and spiteful towards everyone if they speak to his wife.' Parker was still upset about the breakdown of his marriage and Brinkley had recently visited his wife and mother-in-law.

Brinkley appeared at Croydon Borough Police Court the following morning, and it took days for witnesses to give their evidence before magistrates.

Unfortunately for Brinkley it became impossible to maintain his assertion that he had not been in Croydon on the evening before the deaths. He was seen at Chelsea Station by a friend who had known him for seven or eight years, and the friend was able to testify that Brinkley had boarded a train bound for Croydon at about six o'clock on the evening of 20 April. Eighteen-year-old John Holden was employed by Mrs Hardstone to work in her off-licence and he remembered Richard Brinkley coming into the shop to buy a bottle of oatmeal stout. The bottle Brinkley took to Churchill Road was stamped with Hardstone's label. Although Mrs Hardstone served him, it was the young man who recognized him. He remembered him clearly, he told police, because he had quibbled over paying the 2d. deposit on the bottle. He stuck in John Holden's memory so well that he was able to identify him from among ten other men at the police station.

Added to this was the evidence of Mr William Vale. Vale, who lived in South Norwood, was a member of the Pharmaceutical Society, and had been introduced to Richard Brinkley by his son, Arthur Vale, in June the previous year. Brinkley had told him that he needed to buy some poison to put down a dog, and he asked specifically for prussic acid. Mr Vale remembered that Brinkley mispronounced the name, calling it 'proosic' acid. He sold him a quantity of prussic acid sufficient to kill a dog, and a day or two later Brinkley returned, saying he had spilled the first bottle and therefore needed some more. Other witnesses were able to inform the court that Richard Brinkley had never owned a dog.

The arrest and his period on remand were taking their toll on Brinkley. As the magistrates' hearing stretched into days the court reporters noticed the deterioration in his appearance. 'Throughout the whole of the hearing [he] scarcely moved,' reported the *Croydon Advertiser*. 'That his mental sufferings are great was evidenced by the haggard expression on his face, and this was somewhat added to by the short beard which he has grown during the remand.'

There was sufficient evidence to send him for trial and he was scheduled to appear at the assizes in Guildford in July 1907.

But if Richard Brinkley put prussic acid in the bottle of oatmeal stout, what were his motives? He barely knew the Becks; they could not possibly have been his intended victims. But they had drunk from the bottle of stout left in their living room and paid a very heavy price. The poison was, of course, intended for Reginald Parker. And the reason for this centres on a convoluted story involving the will of an elderly lady named Johanna Maria Blume.

Mrs Blume, who was well into her seventies, had a property in Maxwell Road, Fulham. She lived with her granddaughter, Augusta, whose mother had died some years earlier. Her only other close relative was an unmarried daughter, Caroline, who had several children by the man with whom she lived. Mrs Blume was said not to approve of this relationship.

For some time Richard Brinkley had been paying Mrs Blume regular visits, calling her 'granny' and kissing her affectionately on arrival and departure. This was kindness indeed for a man not renowned for his philanthropy. Sadly, it seems, his motives were less altruistic: he had his eye on Mrs Blume's property. On 16 December she apparently signed a will, making Richard Brinkley her sole beneficiary. He stood to gain her house in Fulham, her furniture, all her stocks and savings, in short everything she had, the whole estate being valued at approximately £725. This was a significant sum for a carpenter in 1907. Whether he tricked her into signing the will, or whether he talked her into it is unclear. The granddaughter was aware that her grandmother had signed a paper relating to a Masonic outing, but she knew nothing about a will. Two days after signing the will Mrs Blume was dead, although her granddaughter had left her in seemingly good health in the morning. The death was not seen as suspicious at the time and therefore no post-mortem was carried out. Brinkley visited the doctor himself to make sure that the dear lady was not 'cut up', as it was not what she would have wanted, he insisted. Perhaps it was not what Brinkley wanted, either. And so the inquest jury happily accepted the doctor's view of 'apoplexy' as the cause of death.

The will had apparently been witnessed by two gentlemen: Henry J Heard and Reginald C Parker. The only difficulty was that Reginald Parker had no idea that he had signed any such document. He had put his signature to various papers, including papers that he had drawn up for Brinkley himself, and one that related to a Masonic outing, the same outing that Mrs Blume had put her name to. But he had never met Mrs Blume and had not witnessed her will, although he agreed that the signature did indeed look like his. But now the will was being contested by Mrs Blume's daughter, Caroline.

Richard Brinkley had at first acted with supreme confidence in taking possession of Mrs Blume's property in Maxwell Road, Fulham. He informed Mrs Blume's daughter and granddaughter that they were entitled to nothing, brandishing the will that he drew from his pocket, and even began selling some items of furniture. When Caroline Blume's solicitor started proceedings to dispute the will, he tried a different approach. First he used his powers of persuasion to try to talk Caroline out of taking legal action. And when she proved adamant he played his trump card

– he proposed. 'It was your mother's wish that I should marry you,' he told her, 'and I should settle the property.' She laughed at his offer and continued with her action to contest the will.

So it was now imperative that the will should be proven legally sound. And if Reginald Parker denied ever having formally witnessed Mrs Blume's will, this would be impossible. Richard Brinkley stood to lose everything he had worked to gain, and this he was not prepared to do. Reginald Parker had to be removed from the picture. This was the motive that was presented to the jury at the Surrey Assizes in Guildford in July 1907.

Brinkley continued to claim that the will was sound and that he had never visited Croydon. He claimed, in tears, that on the evening of 20 April he was in the King's Road, in a shop belonging to a Mr Snapper, until about seven o'clock, when he went straight home. These two assertions should have been relatively easy to prove to the court: Henry Heard, the co-signatory to the will, could have testified that Reginald Parker had formally and properly witnessed the will, and Mr Snapper could have testified that Brinkley had been in the King's Road until seven o'clock on 20 April. Neither gentleman was called by the defence. Everything was based on Brinkley's word alone.

The case was a curious one since murder must involve the element of intent to kill, and there was nothing to suggest that Richard Brinkley had ever intended to kill Mr and Mrs Beck. But as the judge informed the jury in his summing up, 'If he took poison to that house with the intention of poisoning someone, it did not matter who, then he was guilty.' It took the jury fifty-five minutes to decide that Richard Brinkley was indeed guilty of the murder of Richard and Anne Beck, and of the attempted murder of Daisy Beck, their daughter, and of Reginald Parker. He was sentenced to death.

The general opinion of those present at the trial was that Brinkley deserved to die. Indeed the editorial of the *Croydon Advertiser* commented that 'the world is rid of a miserable man.' But there was one person who felt for him at this awful moment:

Amidst the crowded Court there appeared to be only one person who pitied the prisoner in his unfortunate position, and by whom the passing of the death sentence was keenly felt, and that was Caroline Blume, the daughter of Mrs Blume, at whose instance the will was being contested. During the time the jury was absent she sat in the well of the Court silently weeping, and when the judge uttered the dread words of the death sentence she was so overcome that a friendly constable had to assist her from the building. Outside she almost collapsed, and it was some short time before she was able to move away.

It was, of course, Caroline's action in contesting the will that had sparked off the whole series of events, but her reaction in court speaks either of a very tender heart, or of a lady who had fallen for the charm of the curious Mr Brinkley.

CHAPTER 21

A Jekyll and Hyde Case:
Edward Finch, 1895

One of the phases of his insanity was that he had a dual identity.

hirty-year-old Edward Finch remarked to his fiancée only a few days prior to his death that 'a fair madman' had just been transferred to Cane Hill Mental Hospital, where he worked as an attendant. It was a strange statement to make, but the man he was referring to, George Guy, seemed rather more volatile than most of the other residents. He had very recently been moved from a mental institution in Colney Hatch where he had spent the previous five years, and his removal certificate described him as having 'suicidal tendencies'. He was watched carefully and the attendant in charge of his ward was warned in writing that he was 'a dangerous patient and suicidal, and was not to be trusted with knives'. It was the general belief, however, that he was a danger to himself rather than to others.

On Monday, 16 September 1895 about a hundred patients were taking exercise in the number two airing court, under the

Cane Hill Asylum. Croydon Local Studies Library

watchful eyes of three attendants. This was a normal ratio. The courtyard was enclosed by hospital buildings and in the centre was a garden bed planted with trees and shrubs. The greenery made the courtyard more pleasant, but it also made it more difficult for the attendants to see all the patients all the time. Among the hundred men taking exercise was George Guy. There had been nothing suspicious about his behaviour that afternoon, nothing to alert the attendants to what was to follow.

As Guy reached the side of the courtyard walled in by the men's infirmary, he made a sudden dash for a waste-water pipe that ran from the rooftop to the ground. Using the joints and wall brackets as footholds, he scaled the pipe, narrowly escaping the attendant who tried to grab him by the feet. By the time the alarm whistles were blowing and other attendants were rushing in from the wards, Guy was on the roof. The courtyards on either side of the roof were cleared of patients, and the attendants spread out around the building in the hope that they might be able to break his fall if he should jump or slip.

In the time it took to organize the attendants on the ground, Guy had been busy pulling the slates off the roof and creating neat piles around him. He began throwing them at the men on the ground. They called to him, urging him to come down, but he refused. 'You're all murderers,' he shouted. 'I've been poisoned and you'll all be sent to penal servitude for life.' He was pacing up and down the flat leaded section of the roof, a broken slate in one hand and, in the other, a wooden plank that he had ripped up from the roof. After a time the attendants brought in fire ladders, placing them at intervals along the walls. The hastily drawn up

Cane Hill Asylum. Croydon Local Studies Library

plan was that several attendants should climb the ladders simultaneously and make a rush at George Guy. The assistant medical officers who were in charge of the operation, Dr Boycott and Dr Pope, decided against using fire hoses to get Guy down, as the water would make the rooftop dangerously slippery. Aware that the situation was dangerous anyway, they gave no orders to the attendants to climb the ladders – they relied solely on volunteers.

As the men started to climb they were pushed back by the hailstorm of slates that Guy was throwing down at them. Even with their helmets it was a perilous undertaking for the attendants. It took several attempts before anyone reached the top. The first man to make it was Edward Finch. The *Croydon Times* described what happened:

> *Finch made more than one attempt to get up the ladder, but was driven back by the slates thrown at him by Guy. Eventually he succeeded in reaching the roof, and made a rush at Guy, who struck at him with the board he had in his hand, smashing in his helmet. Finch staggered and slipped, and caught hold of Guy's knees. Guy then struck him again, and he fell on his back on the flat part of the roof.*

Other attendants had now reached the scene to secure Guy. Dr Boycott attended Edward Finch, who was lying unconscious

Aerial view of Cane Hill Asylum. Croydon Local Studies Library

REGISTER OF MALE ATTENDANTS.

Date of entering upon Office.	NAME.	Age.	Office or Department to which appointed.	Salary or Wages £	Revision of Salary or Wages during current year.		Date of Leaving.	Cause of leaving and observations.
					Date from which payable	Amount £		
1873								
1869 16	John Ramsey Shannon	26	2d Class Att.	531	Aug 18.74 76			
Nov 12	Henry Beadle	25	"	"				
14	Charles Raymond Francis	27	"	"			29. 6. 95	Voluntarily
29	William Ernest Allen	27	"	"	Sep. 19 71			
Dec 19	Edward Finch	27	"	£30		2	Sept. 18.875	Last

with severe head injuries. After Finch had been taken from the roof to his own room Dr Boycott examined the injury more closely and found that the skull had been fractured. Finch never regained consciousness. He lived for two more days, and on Wednesday, 18 September a surgeon from St Thomas's Hospital came to perform a procedure known as trepanning, whereby a hole is made in the skull to release the pressure inside. Edward Finch died later that day in the presence of his fiancée and his family.

The police were now faced with a dilemma. Should George Guy, already certified as insane, be arrested for the murder of Edward Finch, or should he simply be left in custody at the asylum with no trial? The inquest returned a verdict of wilful murder against George Guy, but there seemed little point in pursuing the case in the courts. The *Croydon Review* discussed the issue:

> *It was absurd to ask him if he had anything to say, or why he should not be committed for trial. The obvious result will be his re-committal to a lunatic asylum, not necessarily as a criminal as he was mad when he fatally injured the unfortunate warder. According to the statement of the doctor, one of the phases of his insanity was that he had a dual identity, a sort of 'Dr Jekyll and Mr Hyde', and before the magistrates, almost with dramatic effect, he pointed to himself and said, 'It was not this man, he would not do such a thing,' evidently implying that he had a benevolent and malevolent identity.*

Guy was being held in his room at the asylum, under police guard. He was allowed to leave the room for short periods of exercise, but his clothes were taken from him on his return to the room to prevent any attempts to escape. Inspector Lemmey was sent to Cane Hill Hospital on 28 September to escort him to Croydon, so that he might appear before the magistrates. Guy seemed cheerful, but said he could not help them; he knew nothing about the incident. His hearing before the magistrates was a strange affair. No one wanted to state that Guy was fit to plead or that he understood the difference between right and wrong. It was a meaningless process. Only George Guy seemed certain about the need for a trial. 'If I have got to die,' he said, 'I have got to die. I am a sane man. I am quite sane and they have no right to keep me – shutting me out of the world.'

The case was referred to the Central Criminal Court, where, as anyone might have predicted, he was found unfit to plead. The Old Bailey records state that:

In the case of George Guy (35), indicted for the murder of Edward Finch, upon the evidence of Mr George Edward Walker, surgeon to Her Majesty's Prison of Holloway, the jury found him to be insane and unfit to plead, and he was ordered to be detained until Her Majesty's pleasure be known.

CHAPTER 22

Deadly Love Triangle: Charlotte Alice Harber, 1928

A single knife wound caused Alice's death.

n the afternoon of Thursday, 6 September 1928, William Benson walked into Coulsdon Police Station and spoke to duty officer PC Harrington with disarming simplicity. 'We want an ambulance,' he said. 'I have just killed my girl.'

PC Harrington looked at the calm, composed young man standing before him, and asked if he understood what he was saying.

'Yes,' Benson replied. 'I have done it to keep her from going back to her husband.'

'How did you do it?'

'I stabbed her.'

'Where is she?'

'Up Stoat's Nest Road.'

An ambulance was called to the police station so that PC Harrington and William Benson could direct the driver. As they neared the cart track that leads to Coulsdon Golf Course, Benson pointed to the body of a woman lying on the grass with her arms stretched out. The left side of her chest was covered in blood and there was no sign of life. A few yards away a very young child was crying in his pushchair.

William Benson was just twenty-five years old. Four years earlier he had met Sidney Harber when they were both working at the Walls Ice Cream Factory. But by February the following year Benson had lost his job and Harber offered to put him up at his home in Malden Road, Kentish Town. It was an extraordinarily generous offer since Sidney Harber lived in just one room with his wife Charlotte Alice, known as Alice, and a young child. A second child followed four years later. A situation where three adults live in one room must inevitably create certain tensions. And these tensions were stretched to breaking point in August 1926 when Harber returned home one day to find Benson 'seducing' his wife, as he described it. Up to this point Harber had regarded Benson as a brother, but this incident pushed him too far. He ordered Benson to leave the house immediately and then turned violently against his wife.

The most extraordinary thing is that a few days later Harber allowed Benson to return to the bed-sit in Malden Road. It is hard to imagine what might have made him relent in the face of such a blatant betrayal of his trust. But perhaps it was Alice who engineered the return – she certainly seems to have been falling in love with Benson. And she had a hold over Sidney Harber: he later told police that she often threatened to commit suicide and take the children with her. Did she pressurize Harber into taking Benson back in this way?

The situation was not a happy one. There were frequent quarrels between Sidney and Alice Harber over her growing affection for Benson: in Harber's words, 'It caused some blows between me and my wife.' Several months later Harber again threw Benson out of the bed-sit because 'I gathered he was getting too fond of her again.' This time Alice and Benson set up a different domestic arrangement that enabled them to spend time together. Alice took a room in Bayswater in the name of Mrs Benson, explaining to the landlady, Mrs Triebel, that it was for herself, her husband and their two children. She spent her days with Benson and usually went home at night. The children rarely went to Bayswater with her.

A double life had begun and far from easing the emotional tension, it seems to have intensified it, with Benson finding it increasingly difficult to watch Alice return to her husband at the end of each day. Harber, meanwhile, remained in ignorance of the room in Bayswater. A letter written by Alice to Benson shows how possessive the latter was becoming and gives an insight into her almost childlike open-heartedness. This is the letter just as she wrote it:

My Dear Bill

   I got home quite safe and everything was alright so don't worry over me and as for doing what you said is the last thing I could ever think of doing and would rather put a knife through him than give myself to him. Well Darling I will be over on Wensday so please leave key in the safe place so I can get in for Darling I can't resist the temptation in waiting till Saturday. Well love S is trying to be nice when all the time he is working behind my back but never mind. . . . Well Darling I am longing for Wensday to come so as to see you again for a few hours and be alone together in each others arms again for I love you more than my own life. I will always cover you and your life for I can't possible life with out for I have learnt that much and as forgetting you is the last thing I could think of doing for if it should ever come to that you know what will happen then but Darling you need not worry about that for it will never come to that for we love each other to much for that to happen.

Coulsdon Golf Course. Purley Reference Library Collection, Croydon Local Studies Library

In late August Alice went to a convalescent home at Littlestone-on-Sea with the younger of her two children. There is no record of what she was convalescing from, whether a physical ailment or mental stress, but she did not return to Malden Road. Instead she left the convalescent home and arranged to meet William Benson on 5 September. They took a room on Euston Road for themselves and Alice's fourteen-month-old son, and spent the night together. They left between ten and eleven o'clock the next day, 6 September 1928. It was Alice's last day.

How or why they ended up on Coulsdon Golf Course was never explained. Perhaps they were looking for a quiet spot to talk over their situation. Perhaps Benson had planned what he would do if Alice refused to leave her husband and wanted to take her to a remote place where they would not be disturbed. He had had the forethought to buy a knife at King's Cross and was wearing it that day in a new sheath fixed to his belt.

Alice did intend to return to her husband and told Benson so. But by 'return' did she mean that she would return to Sidney at night time, just as she had before her stay in Littlestone-on-Sea, or was she threatening to leave Benson permanently? His extreme reaction might suggest the latter, although Alice's letter reveals how jealous he was becoming at the thought of her sleeping with her husband. He gave no complete explanation; he said only that

Coulsdon Golf Course Club House. Purley Reference Library Collection, Croydon
Local Studies Library

he had killed her to stop her returning to Sidney Harber. He
showed no emotion; he showed no remorse.

A single knife wound caused Alice's death. One inch in width,
the knife penetrated the chest wall, caught the edge of her left
lung, and passed right through her heart. It must have taken determination and considerable force to plunge the knife to such a
depth in a single blow. He did not mean her to survive to sleep in
another man's arms.

Despite his plea of insanity at the time the crime was
committed, William Charles Benson was convicted of murder at
the Old Bailey, and hanged a month later at Wandsworth Gaol.

CHAPTER 23

A Most Heartless Case: Ellen 'Nellie' Saddington Woods, 1885

By now her voice was almost too small to be heard.

Mary Ann Woods was desperate. She was starting to run out of options. She earned just £15 a year and it cost her 4 shillings a week to have her illegitimate daughter, Nellie, cared for. As if the expense were not bad enough, now her problems were made worse: no one wanted to take in Nellie at all, not for money and not out of pity. If she didn't sort out the problem soon she would lose her own job: her employer would only allow her so much time off work, especially for a child that the world believed to be her niece. It would simply have been too disgraceful to admit that six-year-old Ellen, known as Nellie, was her own natural daughter. Even Nellie called Mary 'aunt' rather than 'mother'.

Mary worked as a domestic servant at the *Sun*, a public house in Lamb's Conduit Street, London. According to her employer, Thomas Whaley, 'she was exceedingly well-behaved, and we had every confidence in her.' She had worked for them both before and after her pregnancy, seven years in all, but they had no idea that she'd had a child – it was easier than we might imagine to conceal a pregnancy beneath the loose, full skirts worn by servants in the nineteenth century and Mary probably returned home for the birth. In the early years Mary's mother looked after little Nellie; whether she had died or become too infirm to continue looking after her granddaughter we do not know, but in January 1885, Mary was obliged to find another carer for her daughter. She took her to the sister-in-law of a fellow worker at the *Sun*, a woman named Ellen Watson. But the arrangement was only ever meant to be temporary. They had initially agreed that Mrs Watson would care for Nellie for two or three weeks, and at the end of twenty-one weeks, Mrs Watson told Mary she really would have to make other arrangements. Mary then turned to her sister, Elizabeth, who helped her for several months until she was confined for the birth of her own child in August of that year. It was time for Nellie to move again, and now it was becoming more difficult to find help.

Mary could not take time off work to go to her sister in Huntingdon, and so she wrote to Elizabeth to make arrangements for Nellie's journey. Her letters are peppered with small but endearing mistakes:

> *My dear sister I can't fetch Nellie, so will you kindly send her up on Wednesday afternoon; Mrs Whaley and Miss Metcalf are at the seaside and I don't no when they are coming back. I should riten before but I thought they were coming back yesterday and William's sister-in-law is going to have Nellie until I can get away from hear. You need not send any of her old things with her, dear Lizzie, because Mrs Watkins has lost a little girl so she says her cloths will come in for Nellie, and I shall send you a box off tomorrow Monday so will you ask Jim to call for it Tuesday night and I shall send some money in it; so with fondest love to all . . .*

It is hard to tell whether Mary really had made arrangements for Nellie's care, or whether she had by this time started to form a different scheme. For things did not go to plan. She did not meet Nellie when she arrived in London, as a second letter explains:

> *My dear sister I could not meet Nellie last night but William's sister did, and for anything i no she got hear safe i have not seen her but I shall tonight as Nellie and I and Ted and some of William's friends are going to Southend for a week so if you rite to me before Monday you must address them to Mr Vernon news agent Lamb's Conduit and William will get it and send it on but I will rite and tell you were we are with love . . .*

Again, we do not know how much of this was the truth and how much was to buy Mary some time, for no one had met Nellie when she arrived in London. A police officer found the little girl wandering the streets around King's Cross Station at a quarter to midnight. She was cold, alone and frightened, but perfectly capable of explaining her predicament to the officer, despite her age. He took her first to the police station, and then to the workhouse, where she was taken into care.

The Settlement Officer at Holborn Union Workhouse, Charles Benning, questioned Nellie about her circumstances. We can only imagine the sense of loneliness of a six-year-old girl in such unfamiliar surroundings but it showed in her demeanour: she answered all the officer's questions but by now her voice was almost too small to be heard. He did learn the whereabouts of the aunt in Huntingdon who had put Nellie on the train for London, and on 13 August he visited Elizabeth Carter, Mary's sister, to investigate the child's background. As a result of his conversation with Elizabeth he wrote Mary a letter, telling her that her daughter

The Croydon Workhouse, 1885. Croydon Local Studies Library

was at the workhouse, and requesting that she bring the letter with her when she came to collect Nellie.

The search for a carer was on again. Mary begged an acquaintance who lived in Lamb's Conduit Street to take on Nellie for a short while, longer if possible, and when a reluctant agreement was reached Mary went to the Holborn Workhouse to collect her daughter. 'Were you not surprised at the child not arriving at your house for so long a time?' Mr Benning asked her. Mary said she had been surprised, and had written to her sister in Huntingdon to ask what had become of Nellie, but when questioned by police, Elizabeth Carter said she had received no such letter. Mary seems to have been living from one moment to another, unsure of what her next move would need to be.

So from Friday, 28 August 1885 Nellie stayed with Mrs Johnson in Lamb's Conduit Street, but by Thursday, 3 September the lady had had enough. 'I found the child a trouble,' she later said, and so she wrote to Mary asking her to take her away. Mary's desperation was now hard to hide and she begged Mrs Johnson to keep the child until Monday, 7 September. On that day she told her employer's sister-in-law that she needed to go out that night and that she might not be back until late. She was, in fact, out all night.

On the morning of Tuesday, 8 September, Betsy Barber of Clifton Road, Croydon looked out of her window and saw a child lying in the long grass of the field behind her house. With a neighbour, she went out to the field and saw that the little girl was wearing no dress, hat or shoes, only stockings, a petticoat and drawers, but strangely, there was a white diaper fastened round her neck. Moved at the sight of the cold, trembling child, Mrs

Barber wrapped her in a blanket and carried her indoors. Her neighbour went for the doctor. As Betsy Barber removed the diaper she saw that the girl's throat had been cut and that she was bleeding profusely.

Arthur Mathie, the house surgeon at Croydon General Hospital, examined Nellie. He said:

> *She had a large cut . . . over four inches and a half long – it extended across her throat, and the windpipe was open – the wound was about three-quarters of an inch deep in the deepest part – . . . it was jagged at one part – I have given my evidence that the instrument was not very sharp, but that it was a cutting instrument.*

Nellie had lost a great deal of blood and for at least a week her life hung in the balance. But slowly she began to regain her strength and went on to make a full recovery. Mary, meanwhile, had been arrested for her attempted murder.

When Eliza Islip, the female searcher at Croydon Police Station, examined Mary's undergarments in a private room, looking for blood stains and any physical evidence that might support the charge of attempted murder, she discovered something else. Mary was about eight months pregnant with another baby.

If providing for one child was difficult, it would be much more

so for two. A huge problem for sure, but it hardly explained the callousness of Mary's solution to her difficulty. The newspapers referred to her attempt to murder her own daughter as 'A Most Heartless Case', and it is hard to refute this view. But what exactly was it that made Mary Ann Woods so desperate that she was prepared to kill her own child? The answer lies in the depth of poverty that most of us can

Female Pauper and her child from London Labour and the London Poor *by Mayhew.* Courtesy of Paula McInnes and Bill Sparkes, The Croydon Workhouse

hardly even imagine today. It was a level of poverty that all working people dreaded in the nineteenth century, for it ended in only one place: the workhouse. And before we are too quick to condemn her heartlessness, we need a glimpse of what life in the workhouse was like. The following story illustrates the type of treatment that Mary Ann Woods dreaded being exposed to.

In November 1894 the case of a workhouse inmate hit the headlines. Forty-year-old Eliza Gillard stood accused of 'refractory conduct and refusing to perform her allotted task'. In fact Eliza was ill and found it difficult to carry out the jobs set for her. The report of the Croydon Borough Bench proceedings in the *Croydon Times* told the story:

> *The prisoner said she was made to dress in a cold stone room with the windows open. Her chest was delicate and she had recently been very ill. She complained of the cold – in fact she could not keep a limb still on account of it – and that was why she was punished. The superintendent's wife, on being asked if the windows might be shut while the women dressed, said, 'No, certainly not. You tramps will want a fire next.' That was at six o'clock in the morning. As to the work, it was not true that she did not attempt to do it . . . she did the work in the lavatory, which was nothing more than a stone cell.*

Eliza asked to see a doctor but her request was refused. Instead, as a punishment, she was locked in the men's oakum shed, which was when Eliza rebelled. In her words, she 'was not going to stay there to be killed outright'. The magistrates decided that Eliza was at fault; she had been insubordinate.

In the works of Charles Dickens we learn how the fear of ending up in the workhouse overshadowed the lives of the poor. In his journalistic publication, *Household Words*, he points out that 'We have come to this absurd, this dangerous, this monstrous pass, that the dishonest felon is, in respect of cleanliness, order, diet, and

The ward of a workhouse. Courtesy of Paula McInnes and Bill Sparkes, The Croydon Workhouse

accommodation, better provided for, and taken care of, than the honest pauper.' In his fiction, he brings the horror of the work-house to life. In *Our Mutual Friend* the character of Betty Higden voices her opinion that death is better than life in 'the House', as she calls it – that it would be preferable for her and that it would be preferable for an illegitimate child:

> *Kill me sooner than take me there. Throw this pretty child under cart-horses' feet and a loaded wagon, sooner than take him there. Come to us and find us all a-dying, and set a light to us all where we lie, and let us blaze away with the house into heaps of cinders, sooner than move a corpse of us there!*

These are strong sentiments and ones that we may find hard to understand. But whether Mary Ann Woods truly felt that death was preferable for her daughter than life in the workhouse, or whether her deed was a selfish attempt to spare herself the same fate, we cannot say. But in the end it was not death that spared Mary the fate of the workhouse; it was a sentence of seven years' penal servitude, recommended on account of her previous good character and the 'trials to which she had been subjected'.

Paroxysm of Rage:
Sophia Peckham, 1893

She was as good a little woman as ever broke the bread of earth.

eighbours in Quadrant Road, Croydon were disturbed by yet another argument at number 4. It was between nine and half past nine on the evening of Monday, 2 January 1893, and this time James Peckham had thrown his wife, Sophia, out of the house. They were both slightly the worse for drink and continued their quarrel from either side of the locked front door. Mr Peckham was quite open about his intentions: 'If you come back in,' he told her, 'I'll murder you.'

'Oh no you wouldn't,' said his wife, in a coaxing tone. It was getting chilly and she was anxious to go back inside. Sophia, who at seventy-one was eighteen years her husband's senior, began banging on the door and shouting to be let back in. The next-door neighbours soon grew tired of the noise and sent their servant, Alice Alder, to try to sort it out. She called for a policeman and took a shawl out for Mrs Peckham. The policeman suggested that Sophia find somewhere else to spend the night, with a friend or a neighbour, perhaps, but she was adamant: she was going to get back into her own home. The police officer wandered away and soon after the door opened. As James Peckham allowed his wife back in, he said once more, 'I will murder you.'

As far as the neighbours were concerned, peace had been restored. It was a respectable district consisting of large villa-style houses, and the Peckhams occupied the eight-roomed detached house on the corner of the road. The peace did not last long. Less than an hour later, at twenty

Quadrant Road. Croydon Local Studies Library

past ten, the sound of a gun firing echoed through the neighbourhood and James Peckham walked out of his house. 'Policeman,
here!' he shouted, 'Policeman, come here!' PC George Winders
had been walking the beat in Elliott Road when he heard the
report of the gun. Moving in the direction of the sound, he saw
James Peckham at the junction of Elliott Road and Quadrant
Road, and heard him calling for a policeman. As he approached,
James announced, 'I've shot my wife.'

'No,' said PC Winders in disbelief.

'I have, my bonny boy.'

The officer followed James into the house, and together they
went to the kitchen at the back. The scene was bloody and ugly
and at one glance confirmed Peckham's claim that he had killed
his wife. There was no possibility that Sophia Peckham might still
be alive. Helpfully, James pointed to the double-barrelled shotgun
in the corner of the room. 'I shot her with the right barrel,' he
announced. 'The other barrel is loaded.'

According to the officer, Peckham appeared quite composed
and not in the least unsettled by what had happened: 'He did not
act like a man who realized the awfulness of the deed he freely
admitted having committed.'

PC Winders sought help immediately, and Detective Sergeant
Stemp accompanied Dr Henry Fowler, the divisional surgeon, to
the scene of the crime. The latter recorded his findings in sicken-
ing detail:

> *She was lying with her feet in front of the fireplace and her head in
> the left-hand far corner. She was quite dead but just warm. The
> stockings and dress and the fire-place were covered with blood. The
> skull was completely smashed, the back of the skull being blown back
> and the face forward; the separation of the bones had taken place
> just above the forehead. The base of the skull was completely
> smashed into small pieces; there was no distinguishing one bone
> from another. There was no brain matter in the skull at all. The
> back part of the skull was attached by the scalp only. The greater
> part of the brain was lying in a heap on the floor, and a large piece
> also on the open door of the range. . . . The face was intact, but had
> been blown forward bodily. The eyes, nose and mouth were all
> perfect, and there were no shots in the skin.*

PC Winders advised Peckham that he should consider himself
in custody, to which he made no reply, but sat rocking himself to
and fro, absent-mindedly humming a nautical tune. He became
more talkative at the police station, telling the officers who questioned him about an accident that had caused him to be

Cane Hill Asylum, where James Peckham spent nine months. Croydon Local Studies Library

concussed, and his subsequent stay at Cane Hill Asylum. He told them about his wife's incessant nagging, about the fact that she often struck him, and had done so that night with a pair of tongs; he also remarked that 'she was as good a little woman as ever broke the bread of earth.'

James and Sophia Peckham had only been married for six years. She was both the elder and richer of the two, and the marriage was stormy. Most of their arguments seemed to centre on money – James liked to spend it and Sophia to save it. By trade James Peckham had started as a ship's carpenter, but earned money in later years as a licensed victualler, and this had given him an income of his own. At the time of Sophia's death James was retired, and she had made a will leaving the whole of her property to him, although it seems unlikely that this was at all influential in the case. There was nothing to suggest he had killed her for her money.

The reason he gave for the shooting was her argumentative nature, coupled with a half-hearted suggestion that it had been an accident of sorts. 'I simply say there was no malice in the matter,' he explained. 'It was more by accident than desire. I never put the gun to my shoulder.' His defence counsel went one, some might say ludicrous, step further. 'It might reasonably be inferred,' it was argued, 'that the prisoner was stamping the gun on the floor to drown his wife's voice, and that it went off by accident.' This is somewhat at odds with James's repeated warnings that he would murder Sophia if she came into the house. He had even warned her on previous occasions that their arguments might end in violence. 'If you keep out of my way, I won't hurt you; but if you don't some day I may hurt you,' he admitted saying. There had been no actual reports of violence previous to the killing. In fact, an elderly lady who lived with the Peckhams, a Mrs Woodhams, gave James an excellent character reference. He was, she said, 'a man who would not hurt a worm; and a man with a better heart did not exist'.

The main thrust of the defence, then, was that James Peckham was insane at the time of the killing.

In 1890 Peckham had spent more than nine months at Cane Hill Asylum for a mental condition that was thought to have been induced by heavy drinking. At times he appeared to be recovering, and at others he seemed of unsound mind. Four doctors who attended him at Cane Hill gave evidence at the assize court trial to the effect that James was unable to distinguish right from wrong and that 'his mind was not in a normal condition.' The medical officer at Holloway Prison felt otherwise. He had interviewed Peckham and said he found no signs of insanity. He believed, rather, that the crime had been committed under the influence of alcohol.

Croydon Cemetery, c.1885. Croydon Local Studies Library

There had been several incidents in the past that might indicate some abnormality of mind, and these incidents were related in court. One witness, William Tancock, of Whitehorse Road, Croydon, said that Peckham had been behaving very strangely on Christmas Day, claiming that he was on his way to America and that he had found himself in Liverpool with nothing but his slippers on. And a very bizarre story was told by William Histed, who had visited James Peckham on New Year's Eve. After about an hour Mr Histed tried to take his leave, but James locked the door and forced his visitor to go through weapons drill with a series of firearms. William Histed finally managed to escape in the early hours of the morning by jumping over the garden wall.

The evidence was sufficiently convincing for the jury. They took time to consider their verdict, but decided that James Peckham was insane. He was ordered by the judge to be detained during Her Majesty's pleasure.

Sophia's funeral was a quiet affair. The time of the burial was kept secret since it was feared that crowds might turn up to view the spectacle. The newspapers had given extensive coverage to the murder committed, as they liked to express it, 'in a paroxysm of rage'. In the end only two gentlemen accompanied the hearse to Croydon Cemetery: James's brother-in-law, George Hayman, and William Tancock. And what about James? Did he regret his action? The only expression of regret he ever made was that he had not used the other barrel of the gun to shoot himself too.

CHAPTER 25

Bentley, a Victim of Justice:
PC Sidney Miles, 1952

Let him have it, Chris.

In Croydon's most debated murder case, it is generally acknowledged that there were two victims: the man who was shot on the warehouse rooftop of Barlow & Parker, Police Constable Sidney Miles, and the man who was later hanged for that murder, Derek Bentley.

The details relating to the case have been turned over and over since Bentley's execution in 1953, but what were the facts surrounding the death of PC Miles and why has it become such an issue of controversy?

First, it is important to understand the personalities of two of the protagonists of the crime, Christopher Craig and Derek Bentley. Craig was sixteen years old, had a history of thefts and robberies and a deep grudge against the police for the twelve-year sentence recently passed on his brother Niven for armed robbery.

Advertisement for Barlow & Parker Confectioners. Croydon Local Studies Library

Derek Bentley. Croydon Advertiser

Derek and Iris Bentley as children.
Croydon Advertiser

He was dyslexic and consequently had struggled at school, but from a very young age had developed a fascination with guns. He hero-worshipped his father, who was an excellent shot with an impressive war record, and it was from his father that Craig learned to shoot, although he never mastered the skill to any level of proficiency. As a teenager Christopher had owned, at various times, a surprising total of forty different guns, many of them antique pistols, others working revolvers, and he even traded the weapons at school. He had a gun with him at all times, wherever he went. Craig had a lively imagination as a child and as he grew older indulged in fantasies of gun battles with the police, fantasies fuelled by the gangster films he loved to watch at the cinema.

Derek Bentley was nineteen at the time of the killing. He, too, had had a troubled past in terms of his education and in acquiring a juvenile police record for theft. But although his family was poor, it was also loving and supportive. Derek had had several epileptic fits as a very young child, and these returned following a fall in 1945 at the family home in Fairview Road, Norbury. The fits were to stay with him for the rest of his life. From the age of twelve he attended Norbury Manor School, but struggled to keep up with lessons, more often than not playing truant. He was convicted of several minor thefts and was sent to Kingswood Approved School near Bristol, where his parents visited him regu-

Derek Bentley. Croydon Advertiser

larly. It was here that tests were conducted to ascertain Bentley's learning abilities: with an IQ of 66 he fell into the category of 'feeble-minded' and his reading age was assessed as being that of a four-and-a-half-year-old. Overall his mental age was rated as below that of an eleven-year-old, although by this time he was seventeen. When called up for National Service in 1952, he was rejected on the grounds of mental incapacity.

Christopher Craig and Derek Bentley knew each other from school, although with a three-year age gap they were unlikely to have been close. But by May 1952 they were friends, in spite of the Bentley family's disapproval of the relationship. Craig was a familiar sight in Norbury, and everyone knew his confident swagger and his American drawl aped from the gangster films. It might be that he was drawn to Bentley as an accomplice because he was impressed by the fact that Bentley had been to an approved school – Craig's idolized brother Niven had also been sent to an approved school. Or it might simply have been that Bentley was easy to manipulate.

Derek Bentley lost his job as a road sweeper in July 1952. He had started out as a dustman, but found this hard to manage. When he lost his job with Croydon Council, Bentley withdrew into himself. He was suffering from the headaches that seemed to go hand-in-hand with his epilepsy, and he spent a great deal of his time doing odd jobs around the family home in Fairview Road. On Sunday, 2 November 1952 Derek Bentley went to the Astoria Cinema in Streatham, where his sister Iris worked as an usherette. He saw Betty Grable in *The Lady from the West* but left part-way through the film because he had 'one of his headaches'. Later that evening Bentley went out with another friend, Norman Parsley, telling his parents he was just getting some fresh air. But, unknown to the family, there was a plan for that evening. Apparently there was a group of four of them who were going to break into a butcher's shop in Croydon. Bentley had worked at one time for this particular butcher and had stolen a bunch of keys, which would not only give them access to the shop, but also to the safe. However, when they reached the shop there was a light on, and two of the group of would-be burglars decided to leave. Craig and Bentley remained.

In Craig's pocket was a gun. It was a .455 Eley service revolver that he had modified in the workshop of the garage where he was now employed, by cutting down the size of the barrel, making it easier to carry. Craig liked to refer to it as his Colt 45. Whether Bentley knew that Craig was carrying the gun at this point is uncertain: he later claimed that he had not known and his sister had often heard him say that he didn't want to have anything to do with guns, but anyone who knew Craig knew that he was likely to have a weapon on him.

Thwarted in their plans to break into the butcher's shop they scouted round for another opportunity and saw the warehouse of Barlow & Parker Confectioners in Tamworth Road. But they had been spotted. From a house on the other side of the street, neighbours watched them climb over the gate, and even as Bentley and Craig were working out how to break into Barlow & Parker, DC Fairfax from Croydon Police Station was learning about their activities. Mrs Alice Ware later said:

> *At about 9.15 p.m. on 2 November 1952 I was in my daughter's bedroom and I looked out of the front bedroom window. My house is exactly opposite the entrance to Messrs Barlow & Parker's warehouse. When I looked out of the window I saw two men walk from the side passage entrance of Messrs Barlow & Parker's premises. They went to the kerb of the pavement. I saw the shorter of the two men climb over the metal gate at the side of the premises and the other man remained on the pavement and looked up and down. After two or three minutes I saw the other man climb over the gate.*

The police were on the scene within four minutes.

The official version of events is that DC Fairfax and PC Harrison were the first to arrive, closely backed up by PC McDonald and PC Sidney Miles. By now Craig and Bentley were on the rooftop, having failed to find an entry point into the building from the ground floor. This was to be the scene of the drama that followed.

While PC Miles went to find the key-holder of the warehouse, the other three officers followed Craig and Bentley to the rooftop. DC Fairfax was the first to climb up a drainpipe to reach the roof, and when he saw the men about 15 yards in front of him he identified himself as a police officer and told them to give themselves up. They backed away towards the lift shaft and Craig told Fairfax in no uncertain terms that if he wanted them he would have to come and get them. The struggle began.

DC Fairfax grabbed Bentley first, and, still holding on to him, reached out to take Craig. PC Harrison was the next to arrive and it was at this point, according to the officers, that Bentley shouted the crucial words: 'Let him have it, Chris.' PC McDonald was still struggling to get up the drainpipe, but he says he heard the words when he was halfway up. It was a pivotal sentence and heavily influenced the outcome of the whole case. Did Derek Bentley ever utter those words? We will examine that in due course.

By now Craig was brandishing his gun, and Bentley had managed to break free of Fairfax. There was a shot and DC Fairfax was hit in the shoulder. Although he was injured, Fairfax was made of stern stuff, and without hesitating punched Bentley, dragged him to the head of the stairs and, lying low to the ground, used him as a shield against further shots from Craig. There he searched Bentley and found a knife, and the knuckleduster that Craig had given him as a gift earlier that evening. The knife was of the type regularly used by burglars to force open window catches. Bentley was now utterly passive and made no further attempts to break free.

PC McDonald was less agile than his colleagues and it had taken him several attempts to climb the drainpipe that Fairfax had used. As McDonald reached the parapet he needed Fairfax's help to get over; Bentley, in those moments, was simply standing by, unbound in any way and making no move to escape. The officers were assessing the situation. Fairfax told PC McDonald that he had been shot, to which Bentley added, according to McDonald, 'I told the silly bugger not to use it.'

All the focus was now on capturing Craig, but he was resisting arrest and fulfilling his dreams of a gangster-like shoot-out at the same time. The burglary had failed before it had even begun and if Craig and Bentley had given themselves up when the police first arrived it would have been a relatively minor matter. But Craig was caught up both in the drama of the moment and in his hatred for the police.

PC Miles had returned with the keys to the warehouse, and he made his way up through the building to reach his colleagues. Sidney Miles unlocked the door at the head of the internal stair-case, opened the door and was shot through the head. He died immediately. His fellow officers pulled his body to safety but there was nothing anyone could do. The bullet had passed cleanly through his skull, entering at the innermost point of his left eyebrow and exiting at the back of his head.

Craig yelled out, 'Is he dead?' And according to Craig's later testimony, it was Bentley who replied, 'Yes he is, you rotten sod.'

The police decided it was time to take Bentley away from the scene. They pulled him down the staircase, and as he left he called out to Craig, 'They're taking me down.'

By now back-up had arrived at street level, and police weapons had been brought to the scene; although he was injured, it was Fairfax who took a weapon and returned to the rooftop. It was the shoot-out that Craig had always wanted. Fairfax called out to him to drop his gun, and warned him that he, too, was armed. 'Come on then, copper. Let's have it out,' was Craig's reply. Fairfax shot twice.

Craig was not going to wait to be either shot or arrested. It looked as though he was out of ammunition, and in a final dramatic gesture he dived head first off the rooftop. His fall was broken by the wooden structure of an outhouse in a garden to the rear of the building. His injuries were serious but not fatal, as revealed by the doctor who attended him at Croydon General Hospital, Dr Douglas Freebody:

He has a fracture of the dorsal spine at the level of the seventh dorsal vertebra. He also has a fracture dislocation of the sternum or breastbone. As a result of the injuries he also had a contusion of the chest. He also had a fracture involving the lower end of the forearm.

Craig was charged with murder at his hospital bedside at 11.30 that night. 'Is the copper dead?' he asked. 'How about the others? We ought to have shot them all.'

Bentley, meanwhile, was

Rear of Barlow & Parker's warehouse, with a line showing where Christopher Craig jumped from the roof. Croydon Local Studies Library taken to Croydon Police Station. In the police car on the way there he was reported to have said, 'I knew he had a gun but I didn't think he would use it. He has done one of your blokes in.' Bentley made a full statement to the police. He did not mention the plans for the butcher's shop and he said that the others in the group had left before he and Craig caught the bus into Croydon. Detective Chief Inspector John Smith read the statement back to Bentley and asked him to sign it and to affirm that it had been as he had dictated. Bentley struggled to write, managing 'tis as be' for 'this has been', before DS Shepherd offered to write on his behalf, 'This statement has been read to me and is true.' He then made several attempts at his signature, managing nothing more than 'Derk' for 'Derek' the first time. At 5.30 he was told he was going to be charged with murder, to which he replied, 'Chris shot him. I hadn't got a gun. He was with me on the roof and shot him between the eyes.'

From his hospital bed and under constant guard, Craig continued to pour out his loathing of the police, reliving the shoot-out as though it were a film that played out in his head, with him in the starring role. 'Is he dead?' he asked one officer in the early hours of the morning. 'That copper. I shot him in the head and he went down like a ton of bricks.' Then, according to another officer a day or two later: 'If I hadn't cut a bit off of the barrel of my gun I would probably have killed a lot more policemen. That night I was out to kill because I had so much hatred inside me for what they done to my brother.' And to another: 'You are coppers. Ha. The other one is dead, with a hole in his head. I'm all right. All you bastards ought to be dead.' It sounded venomous, and the police had to listen, still angry and grieving over the death of their colleague.

Christopher Craig was sixteen and could not be hanged for the murder of PC Sidney Miles. Derek Bentley, at nineteen, could. Yet it was Craig who carried the weapon, Craig who fired at the police, and at the time of the killing Bentley was technically in police custody. The law states that if two people commit a crime with a common purpose, then they are equally responsible for the outcome of that crime. Therefore if it could be shown that Craig and Bentley were acting with a common purpose on the night of 2 November 1952, then they were equally responsible for the death of Sidney Miles, at least in the eyes of the law. This is why the words 'Let him have it, Chris' were so vital to the prosecution case. It showed that Bentley was inciting Craig to violence, despite the fact that he carried no gun himself, and it established a common purpose even though the phrase was allegedly said at a much earlier point in the evening, before PC Miles was even on the roof. This argument was reinforced if it could also be shown that Bentley knew that Craig was armed. Prosecuting counsel explained that the phrase

was spoken to a man who he, Bentley, clearly knew had a gun. That shot began a gun fight, in the course of which Miles was killed; that incitement . . . covered the whole of the shooting thereafter, even though at the time of the actual shot which killed PC Miles, Bentley was in custody and under arrest.

So, first, did Bentley know that Craig was carrying a loaded gun? It is unlikely that he did not know Craig was armed. Craig was always armed. But it is quite possible that because he was always armed, it would not have been uppermost in Bentley's mind. He may never have considered the possibility that Craig would actually use his gun. The police claim that Bentley told them, 'He's got a .45 Colt and plenty of bloody ammunition too.' Bentley's sister Iris suggested in her book *Let Him Have Justice*, that he would have said 'Colt 45' rather than the more technical '.45 Colt'. Indeed, Craig claimed that it was he who told the police he had a Colt 45, not Bentley at all. It was, after all, the way he liked to refer to the weapon. But someone must have mentioned it at some point. If the police were totally fabricating this piece of evidence, they would have had no reason to use the word 'Colt' at all; it was a .455 Eley. The crucial question remains: who said it, Craig or Bentley?

The second point of contention, whether Bentley at any time used the words 'Let him have it, Chris', is more complex. It was certainly an uncharacteristic thing for Bentley to have said – he was used to receiving instructions from Craig, not giving them, as Craig was definitely the dominant personality of the two. Bentley was an unassertive young man, easily unsettled into silence, and never known to use violence. It was never the contention of Bentley's defence counsel that the words were misinterpreted, as some have since argued; that by 'let him have it' he meant not 'shoot him' but 'hand over the gun'. Bentley's defence was quite simply that he had never said those or any other words that might have incited Craig to shoot.

So did Bentley give that fateful instruction, or was it the invention of an extremely frustrated handful of police officers? There are several factors to consider. First, what would have been Bentley's motives for urging Craig to shoot? He had nothing to gain by it, especially since he was being held by Fairfax at the time. Any shot at this point would have placed Bentley at considerable risk. Second, PC McDonald's evidence that Bentley said 'I

told the silly bugger not to use it' conflicts with the argument that
he was inciting Craig to shoot. Third, Bentley's family said that he
never called Craig 'Chris' but 'Kid' or 'Kiddo'. The police would
not have known this. The name 'Chris' appears in Bentley's statement to the police, but that statement, too, did not ring true to his
family. Bentley was incapable of remembering the simplest things,
and he certainly was not able to express himself in fluid, complex
language. The police claimed that Bentley's statement, which was
both detailed and relatively fluent, was made spontaneously, not
as the result of questioning. The Bentley family found this hard, if
not impossible, to believe. Indeed, many experienced police
officers would support this view. Even the most intelligent person
needs guidance in making a statement; the natural tendency to
garble your version of events would result in a meaningless document. It takes the careful questioning of an experienced officer to
produce a coherent statement of the sort that Bentley was
supposed to have made unprompted.

More important than any of this, however, is the suggestion
that there were more than the four officers involved in the rooftop
shoot-out, and that they were not put on the witness stand
because they would not say they heard Bentley use the words 'Let
him have it, Chris'. If this assertion is true, it throws an entirely
new light on the affair. In his book *'Let Him Have It Chris'*,
published in 1990, M J Trow writes of his interview with a retired
police officer, eighty-year-old Claude Pain. Mr Pain was quite
clear, and quite adamant about the events of 2 November 1952.

Iris at Derek's grave. Croydon Advertiser

Iris with the memorial stone which she fought to erect in Derek's memory. Croydon Advertiser

He was also on the rooftop of Barlow & Parker and in the notes he wrote up in his pocketbook afterwards, he made no mention of the words 'Let him have it, Chris'. He told M J Trow, 'I did not write it down because I did not hear it. I did not write it down because it was not said.'

The evidence of PC Claude Pain is detailed and entirely credible. He reached the roof before the first shot was fired and therefore would have been in time to hear Bentley shout to Craig if he had ever done so. He remembered with precision where people were and what was said. Yet PC Pain's testimony was never used; more than that, Fairfax, Harrison and McDonald conspicuously failed to mention that Claude Pain was there at all, even when directly questioned about who was present. It was an omission that casts a long shadow over the evidence of the three officers.

But aside from all the theories and speculation, the fact remains that a teenager of severely limited intellect, who had no previous record of violence, who was in police custody at the time of the shooting, and who did not carry a gun himself was hanged for the murder of PC Sidney Miles. Even Mrs Catherine Miles did not feel that it was right to condemn Bentley to death for the murder of her husband. An appeal was lodged but dismissed on 13 January, and, despite a growing swell of public opinion in favour of mercy, on 28 January 1953 Derek William Bentley was hanged at Wandsworth Prison.

Craig, at sixteen, was given the only sentence permissible by law, that he was to be detained during Her Majesty's pleasure. He served a little more than ten years, after which he married, had

PC Sidney Miles. Croydon Advertiser

children and settled to a life of work as a plumber.

The law changed four years later with the Homicide Act of 1957. Indeed, it is entirely possible that the case of Craig and Bentley was one of several to influence this change in the law. It resulted in the separation of murder cases into two distinct categories: capital, that is one which carries the death sentence, and non-capital. It enabled the court to take into consideration the circumstances of the murder, and if the events that took place on the rooftop of Barlow & Parker had happened after 1957, Derek Bentley would probably not have lost his life.

The Bentley family never gave up the struggle to clear his name and win an official pardon. Their battle was a long and hard one but in 1998 the conviction was finally held to have been unsafe and was quashed. His sister Iris had campaigned relentlessly on her brother's behalf, but she died a year before the conviction was overturned.

The case of Craig and Bentley is one of the best known in modern legal history. But in all the debate over the rights and wrongs of the judicial process, there is one person we should not forget – the forty-two-year-old man who was a reliable comrade to his fellow officers, courteous to all those he helped in the course of his work, a regular and loving family man, PC Sidney George Miles.

Select Bibliography

Anon., *A Letter To Mr Sanxay* (1775)

Anon., *The Life and Trial of Jane Butterfield* (1775)

Bentley, Iris, *Let Him Have Justice* (1995)

Bentley, W G, *My Son's Execution* (1957)

Berry-Dee, C and Robin Odell, *Dad Help Me Please* (1990)

Croydon Oral History Society, *Talking of Croydon* (1990)

Dickens, Charles, *Our Mutual Friend* (1864–5)

Du Cann, C G L, *Miscarriages of Justice* (1960)

Gaute, J H H and Robin Odell, *The Murderers' Who's Who* (1979)

Hall, J G and G D Smith, *The Croydon Arsenic Mystery* (1999)

Honeycombe, Gordon, *The Murders of the Black Museum* (1982)

Janaway, John, *Surrey Murders* (1988)

Johnson, W H, *Surrey Villains* (2004)

McInnes, Paula and Bill Sparkes, *The Croydon Workhouse* (no date)

Morland, Nigel, *Background to Murder* (1955)

Murder Casebook, *The Croydon Poisonings* (1991)

Murder Casebook, *Too Young to be Hanged* (1996)

Paget, Clarence G, *By-ways in the History of Croydon* (1929)

Parris, John, *Scapegoat* (1991)

Philip, Neil and Victor Neuburg (eds), *Charles Dickens: A December Vision* (1986)

Pritchard, R E, *Dickens's England* (2002)

Selwyn, Francis, *Nothing But Revenge* (1991)

Stewart, Frances, *Around Haunted Croydon* (1989)

Trow, M J, *Let Him Have It Chris* (1990)

Wheatley, Dennis, *Drink and Ink* (1979)

Whittington-Egan, Richard, *The Riddle of Birdhurst Rise* (1975)

Yallop, David, *To Encourage the Others* (1990)

Index